Student Applications Book

Great Source Education Group
a Houghton Mifflin Company
Wilmington, Massachusetts

www.greatsource.com

AUTHORS

Jim Burke
Author

Burlingame High School, Burlingame, California
Jim Burke, author of *Reading Reminders: Tools, Tips, and Techniques* and *The English Teacher's Companion,* has taught high school English for 13 years. His most recent books, *Tools for Thought* and *Illuminating Texts: How to Teach Students to Read the World,* further explore reading and those strategies that can help all students succeed in high school. He was the recipient of the California Reading Association's Hall of Fame Award in 2001 and the Conference on English Leadership's Exemplary English Leadership Award in 2000. He currently serves on the National Board of Professional Teaching Standards for English Language Arts.

Ron Klemp
Contributing Author

Los Angeles Unified School District, Los Angeles, California
Ron Klemp is the Coordinator of Reading for the Los Angeles Unified School District. He has taught Reading, English, and Social Studies and was a middle school Dean of Discipline. He is also a coordinator/facilitator at the Secondary Practitioner Center, a professional development program in the Los Angeles Unified School District. He has been teaching at California State University, Cal Lutheran University, and National University.

Wendell Schwartz
Contributing Author

Adlai Stevenson High School, Lincolnshire, Illinois
Wendell Schwartz has been a teacher of English for 36 years. For the last 24 years he also has served as the Director of Communication Arts at Adlai Stevenson High School. He has taught gifted middle school students for the last 12 years, as well as teaching graduate-level courses for National Louis University in Evanston, Illinois.

Editorial:
Design:
Illustrations:

Developed by Nieman, Inc. with Phil LaLeike
Ronan Design: Christine Ronan, Sean O'Neill, Maria Mariottini, Victoria Mullins
Mike McConnell

Printed in the United States of America

International Standard Book Number: 0-669-49507-7
(Student Applications Book)

1 2 3 4 5 6 7 8 9—DBH—09 08 07 06 05 04 03 02

International Standard Book Number: 0-669-49512-3
(Student Applications Book, Teacher's Edition)

1 2 3 4 5 6 7 8 9—DBH—09 08 07 06 05 04 03 02

Table of Contents for Student Applications Book

Lessons

What Is Reading?

Have you heard the saying "every reader reads alone"? It means that you and you alone control your understanding of a text.

What reading is to me

You can train to become a good reader in the same way that an athlete trains. Begin by asking yourself, "What does reading mean to me?"

Directions: Reread pages 26–27 in the *Reader's Handbook*. Then, write your reactions to the following sentences.

Understanding Reading

Reading is working:

Sometimes reading does feel like work. For example, when I'm reading my textbooks, I have to try really hard. I have to focus and think of nothing else. It is just like a workout or basketball practice.

Reading is thinking:

The whole time my eyes are focusing on the words on a page, my brain is churning, churning, churning. I am thinking about what the words mean, about what they remind me of, and about what is going to happen next.

Reading is imagining:

If a book is really, really good, I can be transported to an imaginary land and feel like I'm there, in this place that the book has helped me imagine.

Reading is reacting:

I think this means that when you read, you can't help but react to what the author is saying by thinking: "This is really dumb" or "I wouldn't have done that" or something else. When I read, I react to the plot and characters and then later try to react to the work as a whole.

Reading is enjoying:

Some of the time I enjoy what I read, but some of the time I hate what I have to read. It really depends on the subject and how hard it is. No one likes to read something that is impossible to understand.

How I feel about reading

The *Reader's Handbook* can change how you feel about reading. It can make reading easier and more enjoyable.

Directions: Write your feelings about reading on the lines below. Then, return to this page at the end of the year to find out how your feelings have changed.

This is how I feel about reading: Usually, I like to read. I read parts of the newspaper each day, and I get a bunch of magazines each month. Sometimes I read novels for fun. Mainly I like mysteries and fantasy stories.

This is what I find easiest about reading: I find it pretty easy to get lost in a good book. If I really like what I'm reading, I can shut everyone out and imagine myself in the world the author describes.

This is what I find hardest: Some of my school reading is really, really hard. It seems like the textbooks are impossible to understand. I hate reading them.

Why You 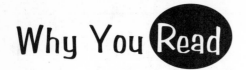Read

In this book, you'll be working to improve your reading abilities. Your first step is to think about the types of things you are asked to read.

Reasons for reading

Why you read often depends on what you read. The *Reader's Handbook* describes the kinds of reading that you might do. Think about why you read these types of texts.

Directions: Review pages 27 and 28 in the *Reader's Handbook*. Summarize the handbook's reasons for reading.

Kinds for Reading

1. Academic reading: This is the reading I am assigned in school. It includes textbooks, maps, graphics, articles, and works of fiction.

2. Personal reading: This is the reading I do on my own. It's websites, newspapers, magazines, novels, and stories for fun, and so on.

3. Workplace reading: At a job, you might have to read memos, emails, or journals. You'll also have to read the rules and policies that an employer gives you.

4. Functional reading: Functional reading is the reading you do when you don't know you're even reading: street signs, road maps, directions, bus schedules, and so on.

> **Summarize what the students in the handbook say about their reasons for reading. Then add your own.**

1. Students' reasons: Reading helps you escape everyday worries and pressures. Reading is an important skill in getting a job. Reading takes you to places you cannot easily go.

2. My reason: I read for entertainment. Sometimes I get sick of TV and video games. I'll pick up a book or magazine and start reading.

What You 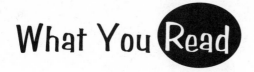 Read

Think about all the things that you read in a given day. Are you shocked to find out that you spend the entire day reading one thing after another?

Kinds of reading

Sometimes you read for school. Sometimes you read for pleasure. Other times, you read without even knowing it.

Directions: Make a list of everything you've read in the last 24 hours. Include everything that you can fit on the page. Then compare your list with a classmate's.

My Reading List

• the back of a cereal box	• directions for a computer game
• the first few pages of a novel	• a note from my mom
• the day and date on my calendar	• an email from a friend
• school papers	• a price tag at the mall
• a recipe for chocolate chip cookies	• the lyrics to my favorite song
• the sports page of the newspaper	• a shoe catalog
• the insert that came with my new toothbrush	• the sign on my brother's door

The Reading Process

A reading process is the steps you follow to read, understand, relate to, and remember a text. Everyone has his or her own habits and rituals when it comes to reading. What are yours?

Your reading process

What do you do before, during, and after reading? Think carefully about all the steps involved and make an outline of them below. Carefully consider why you read better sometimes than others.

Directions: Explain your reading process on the lines below.

Before Reading

I look at the front and back covers and try to guess what the book will be about and whether or not I'll like it. I'll also look at the table of contents and thumb through the pages of the entire work. Usually I'm thinking about what I need to find out as I read.

During Reading

I stop every once in a while and think about what I've read and whether I've understood it. If I'm reading for a school assignment, I take notes sometimes, and I might look up things I don't understand.

After Reading

I think about what I've read and whether or not I liked it. If something wasn't clear to me, I ask a friend. This is especially important if the reading is for a school assignment.

The handbook's reading process

The *Reader's Handbook* describes a reading process that may be different from yours. This reading process is like a road map. It can point you in the right direction and prevent you from getting lost.

Directions: Read pages 38–42 in the *Reader's Handbook*. Then, summarize the reading process on the lines below.

Before Reading

Set a purpose. This means that you need to figure out why you're reading.

Preview the reading. You consider what it is you're reading before you begin. You look at length, difficulty level, vocabulary, organization, and content of the text.

Plan a reading strategy. At this stage you choose a strategy that can help you meet your reading purpose.

During Reading

Read with a purpose. You need to keep your purpose firmly in mind as you read. Look for information that fits your purpose. You need to focus on the information that applies to your purpose and make notes about it.

Connect. You should think about how the text makes you feel, what it reminds you of in your own life, and so on.

After Reading

Pause, reflect, and look back to see if you've met your purpose. Consider again your purpose in reading this piece. Did it meet your original expectations? Did you use the right strategy?

Reread to find out things you missed the first time around. When you reread, you should be able to focus on the most important bits of information.

Remember what you learned. You never know when what you've learned will come in handy later. This is why you need to figure out a way to remember what you've read.

If you get stuck, read "Summing Up" on page 43 of the *Reader's Handbook*.

Reading Know-how

You are making inferences, drawing conclusions, comparing and contrasting, and evaluating everything around you all the time. These skills are the foundation of a good reader.

Thinking Skill 1 Making inferences

When you make an inference, you are making a reasonable guess based on the facts presented.

Directions: Read the following paragraph. Then, use your inferences to help you answer the questions.

Sample Paragraph

The school board holds a special meeting on a Monday night in June. The sign posted at the door says "School Expansion Forum." Inside the meeting room there is a row of high school teachers and several high school students. Some of the high school students are holding signs that say "Vote Yes!" In addition, there are a couple of middle school parents in the audience. At the beginning of the meeting, the president of the school board steps up to the podium and announces, "Tonight, there will be no disruptive behavior. We will follow Robert's Rules of Order for the entire meeting."

My Inferences

The purpose of the meeting is: to discuss a local school expansion.

I know this because: the sign outside the meeting room tells me so.

The school up for expansion is: the high school.

I know this because: there are high school students, teachers, and parents in the audience.

Some of the high school students are: in favor of the proposal.

I know this because: they are holding placards that say "Vote Yes!"

NAME ....

FOR USE WITH PAGES 46–48

Thinking Skill 2 Drawing conclusions

Drawing conclusions means collecting bits of information and then deciding what that information means.

Directions: Read the facts in the left-hand column. Write your conclusions in the right-hand column.

Drawing Conclusions

Facts	My Conclusion
There are high school teachers and students and even middle school parents in attendance.	The issue must be very controversial as parents of future high school students have attended, and the school board president begins by asking for good behavior.
Some of the high school students are holding signs that say "Vote Yes!"	Students are in favor of expanding the school.
The school board president announces that they will be following Robert's Rules of Order at the meeting.	I think that means the meeting will be formal and run according to rules.

Thinking Skill 3 Comparing and contrasting

When you compare and contrast, you think about how things are alike and different. Comparing means noting similarities. Contrasting means noting differences.

Directions: Place two books on your desk. Compare them in terms of size, shape, thickness, and appearance. Put your findings in the Venn Diagram on the next page.

◀ **Venn Diagram** ▶

Write notes that describe Book A here.

Write notes that describe Book B here.

Title: _____
bigger
heavier
lots of pictures

dark cover

Title: _____
smaller
lighter
no pictures

Write what they have in common in the center.

Thinking Skill 4 Evaluating

Evaluating is making a judgment. Very often you do this without even realizing it. You say why you did or did not like a book. You consider whether the writer is as good as everyone thinks. This is evaluating.

Directions: Think about two classes you take in school. Tell which you think will be more interesting. Then explain why.

I think French will be more interesting than math because I'm dying to learn how to speak a foreign language and because I love French movies.

Reading Actively

Active readers are good readers. They ask questions, make predictions, and connect what they are reading to their own lives.

Ways of Reading Actively

Begin by doing an active reading of the following excerpt. Make notes as you go.

<u>Directions:</u> As you read, make notes on the stickies below and on the next page.

"Sea Bubble" from *A Step from Heaven* by An Na

Just to the edge, Young Ju. Only your feet. Stay there.

Cold. Cold water. Oh. My toes are fish. Come here. Fast. Look.

What is it, Young Ju?

See my toes. See how they are swimming in the sea? Like fish.

Yes, they are little fat piggy fish.

Ahhh! Tickles.

Come on. Up. Keep your legs around me. Are you ready to go swim in the waves?

Hold me. Hold me.

I have you. Look over there, Young Ju. See how the waves dance. See? Hold on tight. We are going over there.

No. Stop. Deep water. Go back.

Shhh, Young Ju. Do not be afraid. You must learn how to be brave. See, I have you.

No. No. Go back.

Young Ju, can you be brave? Look, that is only a small wave. Do not worry. I will hold you tight the whole time. Can you try to be a brave girl for me?

I will try.

Good girl. Ready for the wave? Here it comes. Get ready. Up. And down. There, do you still want to go back?

Again. Do it again. Another one.

That is my courageous girl. Hold on to my neck, Young Ju. Here we go. Up. And down.

I am a sea bubble floating, floating in a dream.

1. Mark

Highlight key information about the setting and the characters.

2. Question

Ask a question about the action.

What are Young Ju and her

companion doing?

3. React

Explain your reaction to the writing. It's

different. I know the two characters

are having a conversation, but there

are no quotation marks. But I like the

last line: "I am a sea bubble floating,

floating in a dream."

4. Predict

Predict how you think Young Ju will

feel about the sea from this day

forward. I think she'll love it. She

enjoys being a "sea bubble."

5. Visualize

Make a sketch of the scene here.

6. Clarify

Write your inferences about Young Ju

here. I can tell she's really young.

She seems observant and

creative. She calls her toes

"piggies" and wants to watch them

swim. She is a little timid, but she

is willing to try and be brave.

Reading Paragraphs

Every paragraph has a subject and main idea. Your job as reader is to identify the subject and to understand what the author is saying about it.

Step 1 Read the paragraph.

Begin by doing an active reading of the following paragraph. Make notes as you go.

Directions: Read the following paragraph about the composer Richard Wagner. Make notes on the stickies.

from "The Monster" by Deems Taylor

[Richard Wagner] was a monster of conceit. Never for one minute did he look at the world or at people, except in relation to himself. He was not only the most important person in the world, to himself; in his own eyes he was the only person who existed. He believed himself to be one of the greatest dramatists in the world, one of the greatest thinkers, and one of the greatest composers. To hear him talk, he was Shakespeare, and Beethoven, and Plato, rolled into one. And you would have had no difficulty in hearing him talk. He was one of the most exhausting conversationalists that ever lived. An evening with him was an evening spent in listening to a monologue. Sometimes he was brilliant; sometimes he was maddeningly tiresome. But whether he was being brilliant or dull, he had one sole topic of conversation: himself. What *he* thought and what *he* did.

Highlight/Mark

What repeated words did you notice? He, himself, him, brilliant

Question

Ask yourself a question about the main idea of this paragraph.

My question: What is Taylor trying to say about Richard Wagner?

Step 2 Find the subject of the paragraph.

To find the subject, ask yourself, "What is this paragraph mostly about?"
You can often find the subject by looking at the items on this checklist.

Subject Checklist

☑ the title

☑ the first sentence

☑ key words or repeated words and names

☑ the last sentence

Directions: Answer this question about the paragraph you just read.

What is the Deems Taylor paragraph mostly about? *Richard Wagner*

Step 3 Find the main idea of the paragraph.

The main idea is the point the author is trying to make about the subject.
Sometimes you'll find that the main idea is directly stated. Other times,
you'll need to make inferences about the main idea.

Stated Main Idea

In some paragraphs, the author comes right out and tells you the main
idea.

Directions: Reread the paragraph about Wagner. Highlight the main idea
sentence. Then complete the formula.

Richard Wagner   + *conceited*

(Taylor's subject)   (What he says about the subject)

= *Richard Wagner was very conceited.*

(His main idea)

Implied Main Idea

Sometimes the main idea of a paragraph is implied. This means you'll need
to infer, or make a reasonable guess about, the author's main idea. You do
this by asking yourself, "What is the writer trying to tell me about the
subject?"

Directions: Answer this question about the paragraph.

What else is Taylor trying to tell you about Wagner? *Wagner was a very unlikable man.*

Step 4 Find support for the main idea.

Good writers support their main ideas with convincing facts and details. A Main Idea Organizer like the one below can help you see how the main idea and details in a paragraph work together.

Directions: Complete this organizer. Refer back to the paragraph and your notes as needed.

◄ **Main Idea Organizer**

Subject Richard Wagner		
Detail 1	**Detail 2**	**Detail 3**
He was conceited and thought he was the most brilliant person who ever lived.	He was totally self-absorbed and talked only about himself.	He was dull because he only spoke about himself and how great he was.

Main Idea Richard Wagner was a thoroughly unlikable man.

Reading History

Your job when reading a history text is to find the most important facts and ideas presented in each chapter and figure out what they mean. The tools and strategies you've already read about in the Reader's Handbook *can help.*

Before Reading

Reading history is a matter of being able to organize a body of information that at first might seem overwhelming. Use the reading process strategy of note-taking to help you read a history chapter called "The Supreme Court."

A Set a Purpose

When you read a history text, you are an investigative reporter. Your purpose is to find answers to the 5 W's and H: *who, what, where, when why* and *how.* Before you begin, you have to organize your investigation.

• **Set your purpose by asking the 5 W's and H questions about the chapter.**

Directions: Write down five key questions to ask as you read the following chapter on the Supreme Court.

5 W's and H Organizer

Who	What	Where	When	Why	How
Who are the justices that serve on the Supreme Court today?	What is the purpose of the Court?	Where is its courtroom?	When is the Supreme Court in session?	Why do I need to know about the Supreme Court?	How does someone become a Supreme Court judge?

NAME

B Preview

Always preview a textbook chapter before reading. Look at the title, the study guide or goals box, the first and last paragraphs, and any background information. Also pay attention to repeated or boldface words.

<u>Directions:</u> Preview "The Supreme Court." Write your notes on the stickies.

◄ **Preview Notes** ►

What is the title of the chapter? What is it mostly about?

The title is "The Supreme Court." It is clearly about how the Court works.

What did you notice in the study guide box?

There are a couple of questions that I am going to be expected to answer. I'll look for information that relates to these questions on my careful reading. Also, there are terms to know. Again, I'll watch for these terms during my careful reading.

What did you learn from the first and last paragraphs?

The Supreme Court is the highest court in the U.S. judicial system. It is often called the "court of last resort." One of the most important things the Supreme Court justices do is publish their opinions so that everyone can understand them. The justices who disagree with the majority opinion publish a minority opinion.

What repeated and boldface terms did you notice?

Supreme Court, United States, Constitution, checks and balances, judicial review, appeal, choosing the cases, hearing the cases, ruling on the cases, publishing the opinion.

Chapter 5
The Supreme Court

Key Terms and Concepts

• • • • • • • • • • • • • •

- checks and balances
- judicial review
- appeal
- confirmed
- the rule of four
- brief
- majority opinion
- concurring opinion
- dissenting opinion

Goals

As you read, look for answers to these questions:

1. Why is the Supreme Court often referred to as the "court of last resort"?
2. What are some of the duties of a Supreme Court justice?
3. What does it mean when the Court publishes its "opinion"?

The Supreme Court is the highest court in the United States judicial system. It is the final authority on all cases involving the Constitution, Acts of Congress, and treaties with other nations. For this reason, the Supreme Court is often called the "court of last resort."

The Supreme Court is a key feature of the American system of government. It is the "umpire" in any disagreement between state and nation, state and state, and government and citizen. There is no higher authority in the land.

Stop and Think: What and Why

What is the Supreme Court? Why is it important? Make some reporter's notes on page 26.

Purpose of the Court

The Supreme Court is the only court that is directly mentioned in the United States Constitution. The Framers of the Constitution did this for an important reason. Their goal was to establish a court that would be on equal footing with the president and Congress. In effect, they gave the Supreme Court the right to oversee the work of the other two branches of government. The president and Congress, in turn, were given the right to oversee the work of the Supreme Court.

This three-armed balance of power is an example of checks and balances. **Checks and balances** is a system by which political power is divided among the three branches of government, with each having some control over the others.

The Court's power to oversee the actions of the legislative, executive, and administrative arms of the government is called the power of **judicial review**. Much of the time, the Court uses this power to hear cases in which the constitutionality of a law or action is being questioned. These cases come to the Court in the form of an **appeal,** or request for a new trial.

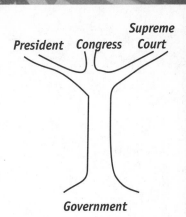

The Court at Work

For the first eighty or so years after the Constitution was ratified, the number of justices serving on the Court fluctuated between eight and ten. This fluctuation caused a great deal of arguing between political parties. To solve the problem, Congress fixed the number of justices at nine in 1869. This number cannot be changed without the approval of the Senate and the House of Representatives.

Today, the Supreme Court is made up of the Chief Justice of the United States and eight associate justices. All nine of the justices serve for life, although Congress has the right to impeach a justice for bad behavior.

Only the president can appoint a justice to the Supreme Court. Before the justice can take a seat on the Court, however, he or she must be **confirmed,** or ratified, by Congress.

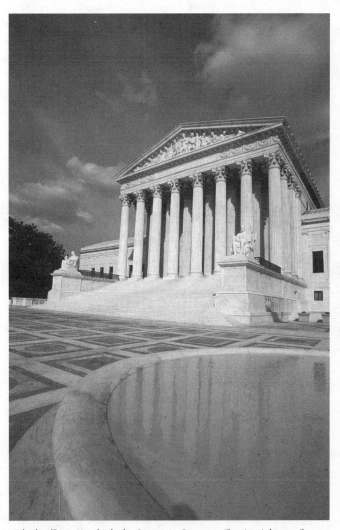

The building in which the Supreme Court resides is nicknamed "The Marble Palace."

Textbooks

Stop and Think: How

How does someone become a Supreme Court judge? Make some notes on page 26.

Supreme Court Justices, 2002

Justice	Appointing President	Year Appointed
William H. Rehnquist (Chief Justice of the United States)	Richard Nixon	1971
John Paul Stevens	Gerald Ford	1975
Sandra Day O'Connor	Ronald Reagan	1981
Antonin Scalia	Ronald Reagan	1986
Anthony M. Kennedy	Ronald Reagan	1988
David H. Souter	George Bush	1990
Clarence Thomas	George Bush	1991
Ruth Bader Ginsburg	Bill Clinton	1993
Stephen G. Breyer	Bill Clinton	1994

Focus Question *Which justice on today's Court has served the longest? Which justice was appointed most recently to the Court?*

Stop and Think: Who

Who are today's Supreme Court justices? Make some reporter's notes on page 26.

Supreme Court Duties

The main duty of a Supreme Court justice is to hear and rule on cases. To fulfill this duty, the Court completes a series of four important steps:

1. Decide which cases will be heard.
2. Hear the oral arguments.
3. Rule on the case.
4. Publish the opinion.

Choosing the Cases. As a first step, the justices must choose the cases they want to hear. Of the thousands of cases submitted to the Supreme Court in a given year, only a few hundred are accepted for review. No case is accepted unless four of the nine justices have agreed that the case should be put on the Court's docket. This is called **"the rule of four."**

Textbooks

Hearing the Arguments. Next, the justices hear the cases. The hearings for Supreme Court cases are public. The Court is in session on Mondays, Tuesdays, Wednesdays, and sometimes Thursdays. Lawyers for both sides of an issue are given a specified amount of time to make their case. To help the justices sort through the complex issues, they are given briefs by the lawyers arguing the cases. A **brief** presents legal arguments, historical materials, and related previous decisions.

Ruling on the Case. As a third step, the justices rule on the cases. They do this by holding private case conferences a couple of times a week. The chief justice presides over each conference and speaks first, usually indicating how he or she intends to vote. Next, the eight associate justices are given the chance to air their own opinions. Lively debates often follow the "polling" of the justices. The debates end with an official vote on the case. In some cases, all nine judges will vote the same way. Other times, the justices split on an issue. When this happens, majority rules.

Publishing the Opinion. As a final step, the justices publish the Court's opinion, which is an announcement and explanation of the Court's decision. If the chief justice has voted with the majority, he or she writes the opinion. If the chief justice has voted with the minority, a senior justice on the majority side will write the opinion. The official opinion of the Court is called the **majority opinion.** Sometimes, another justice or two will write a **concurring opinion** to explain why they agree with the majority opinion. Justices in the minority may publish a **dissenting opinion.** Here, the justice explains why he or she *disagrees* with the majority decision.

Stop and Think: When and Where
When and where does the Supreme Court meet? Make some reporter's notes on page 26.

C Plan

After your preview, make a reading plan. How can you best meet your purpose? The strategy of note-taking can help.

• Note-taking can help you process and remember what you've learned.

During Reading

D Read with a Purpose

Keep your purpose in mind as you read. Remember that you are looking for answers to *who, what, where, when, why,* and *how*.

Directions: Now do a careful reading of the chapter. Make reporter's notes as you go. Record them below. Highlight any important terms or phrases.

Reporter's Notes

The Supreme Court

Who

Nine justices appointed for life by the president

Where

"The Marble Palace"

Why is it important?

It is the ultimate authority in all disagreements between nation and state, state and state, and government and citizen.

What

The highest court in the land

When

On Mondays, Tuesdays, Wednesdays, and some Thursdays, they hear cases. On some Thursdays and Fridays, they hold private conferences to discuss the cases.

How does someone become a Supreme Court Judge?

Only the president can appoint a justice to the Supreme Court. This justice has to be confirmed by Congress.

Reading History

NAME

FOR USE WITH PAGES 73-87

Using the Strategy

Now use your strategy of note-taking to help you achieve your purpose. It's important that you choose the tool that works best for you. Many students find that Key Word or Topic Notes (see page 81 of the *Reader's Handbook*) help them get more from a history chapter. Often, but not always, the key words you use will be the boldface terms.

Directions: Write Key Word or Topic Notes for the Supreme Court chapter.

Key Word or Topic Notes

Key Words	Notes
"court of last resort"	The Supreme Court is called this because it is the final authority on all cases involving the Constitution, Acts of Congress, and treaties with other nations.
Framers of the Constitution	The Supreme Court is the only court specifically mentioned in the Constitution.
three-armed balance of power	The Framers specified that the Court would be on equal footing with the president and Congress. The Court has the right to oversee what the president and Congress are doing, and vice-versa.
judicial review	This is the power of the Court to establish the constitutionality of a law or action.
appeal	This is a request for a new trial.
"the rule of four"	In order for a case to be heard by the Court, four judges must agree to include it on the docket.
majority opinion	The official opinion of the Court
concurring opinion	A document written by a justice that explains why he or she agrees with the majority opinion
dissenting opinion	A document written by a justice that explains why he or she disagrees with the majority opinion

Textbooks

Understanding How History Chapters Are Organized

Most history chapters or articles open with a study guide or goals box. Be sure you understand every term and can answer every question in this box.

• **Use the study guide or goals box to help you figure out what's most important in the chapter.**

Directions: Return to the goals box on page 22. Answer the questions and define the key terms.

1. Why is the Supreme Court often referred to as the "court of last resort"? Because it is the final authority on cases involving the Constitution, Acts of Congress, and treaties with other nations.

2. What are some of the duties of a Supreme Court justice? They choose the cases, hear the cases, vote on them, and write the Court's opinion.

3. What does it mean when the Court publishes its opinion? It means that the Court announces its official decision and why the Court made it.

• checks and balances—system in which political power is divided among the three branches of the government

• judicial review—the power of the Court to establish the constitutionality of a law or act

• appeal—request for a new trial

• confirmed—ratified

• rule of four—four justices must agree to hear a case before it can be placed on the docket

• brief—document that presents legal arguments, historical materials, and related previous decisions

• majority opinion—the official opinion or ruling by the Court

• concurring opinion—a document written by a justice that tells why he or she agrees with the majority opinion

• dissenting opinion—a document written by a justice that tells why he or she disagrees with the majority opinion

E Connect

Connecting to a history text means getting involved in a personal way with the reading.

- **Imagining yourself a part of history can help you make a strong connection to what you've read.**

<u>Directions:</u> Imagine yourself a Supreme Court justice. Which of the four duties discussed on pages 24–25 would you find the most difficult? Why?

The duty that would be most difficult for me would be debating and voting

because I have a really hard time speaking publicly, even in a small group. I might let the other

justices do all the talking, even if I have an important point to make.

After Reading

When you finish reading, take a moment or two to think about what you did and did not understand about the chapter.

F Pause and Reflect

Reflect on your original reading purpose.

- **Ask yourself three important questions about your purpose and what you've learned.**

<u>Directions:</u> Answer these three questions about the reading.

1. Did I meet the reading purpose I set in the beginning? yes

2. Do I know answers to the five W's? yes

3. Do I know enough details to be able to discuss the ideas in the chapter

intelligently? I'm not sure I know every detail.

G Reread

Now return to the text. Reread and look for details you missed the first time around.

- **Use graphic organizers to help you get *more* from your second reading.**

Textbooks

Directions: Use a web organizer to help you group important facts and details from the Supreme Court chapter.

Web Organizer

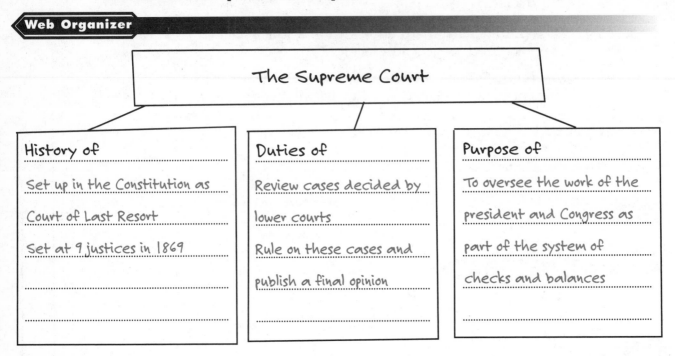

The Supreme Court

History of

Set up in the Constitution as

Court of Last Resort

Set at 9 justices in 1869

Duties of

Review cases decided by

lower courts

Rule on these cases and

publish a final opinion

Purpose of

To oversee the work of the

president and Congress as

part of the system of

checks and balances

 Remember

Good readers remember what they've read.

• **Conducting an "interview" about the subject can help you remember what you've read.**

Directions: Write three interview questions on the lines below. Then, exchange books and have a partner answer them.

Question 1 What is "the Marble Palace"?

Answer: The courthouse building for the Supreme Court

Question 2 What is the title of the head of the Supreme Court?

Answer: Chief Justice

Question 3 How is a concurring opinion different from a dissenting opinion?

Answer: A concurring opinion is written by a justice who agrees with the majority opinion.

....

Reading Science

If you're having trouble understanding science, it may be because of how you're reading the textbook. Good readers know strategies that can help them get more from every chapter.

Before Reading

Use the reading process and the strategy of outlining to help you read and understand a science textbook chapter about igneous rocks.

 A **Set a Purpose**

Your purpose when reading a science chapter is to find out as much as you can about the subject.

• **To set your purpose, turn the title of the chapter into a question.**

Directions: Write your purpose for reading "Igneous Rocks" on the lines below. Then, write what you expect to learn from the chapter.

My purpose: Learn about igneous rocks and find out why they are important.

....

....

Here are three things I expect to learn from this chapter:

1. the characteristics of igneous rocks

....

2. how igneous rocks are formed

....

3. why igneous rocks are important to humans and the environment

....

Textbooks

B Preview

Preview a science chapter first, so that you know what to expect during your careful reading. Pay particular attention to the items on this checklist:

Preview Checklist

☑ title

☑ the first and last paragraphs

☑ headings

☑ boxed items

☑ words in boldface or repeated words

☑ any photos, charts, or pictures

Directions: Skim the science chapter that begins on page 33. Place a check mark beside each feature as you preview it. Then make notes on the Preview Chart below.

Preview Chart

The titles and headings tell me . . .

mostly about igneous rocks: how they are

formed, the role crystals play, and the two

different types of these kinds of rocks

I noticed these boldface words . . .

magma, lava, crystals, extrusive igneous rocks,

intrusive igneous rocks

Igneous Rocks

The art tells me . . .

the difference among igneous,

sedimentary, and metamorphic rocks, and

shows what various igneous rocks look like

I expect to learn . . .

how igneous rocks are formed

the role of crystals

the characteristics of intrusive and

extrusive igneous rocks

Chapter 11.2 | Igneous Rocks

> **Study Guide** •
>
> **Objectives**
> - Learn the origins, features, and types of igneous rocks.
> - Differentiate between extrusive and intrusive igneous rocks.
>
> **Terms to Know**
>
> igneous rocks   crystals
>
> magma   extrusive igneous rocks
>
> lava   intrusive igneous rocks

Did you know that an airplane is made of rocks? It's true! But the rocks you're thinking of are not the rocks an aviation designer uses to build a plane. Instead, the designer uses the iron and other metals that are extracted from several different types of rocks. The most important of these are called igneous rocks.

Igneous rocks are crystalline or glassy rocks that are formed by the cooling and solidification of magma. Igneous rocks, along with sedimentary and metamorphic rocks, make up three principal classes of rocks.

      Igneous   **Sedimentary**   **Metamorphic**

There are three main classes. Most rock is made up of two or more minerals.

The Origin of Igneous Rock

Igneous rocks form when hot melted material, called **magma,** cools and becomes solid rock. Usually this process occurs well beneath the surface of the Earth.

Sometimes, however, magma breaks the surface of the Earth at a volcano and cools above ground. When this happens, the magma is called **lava.** When lava cools, it too forms igneous rock.

Stop and Organize

Make notes in the first section of your outline on page 36.

The Role of Crystals

Which rock material cools above ground: magma or lava?

Crystals, which are solids with atoms arranged in a regular, repeating pattern, are the building blocks of rock. When magma or lava cools from a liquid to a solid, crystals form.

Sometimes the cooling rock material yields crystals large enough to be made into jewelry. Other times, the rock crystals are so tiny that they are invisible to the naked eye.

The length of cooling time determines the size of the rock crystals. Rock material that cools slowly forms larger crystals. Rock material that cools quickly forms smaller crystals.

Stop and Organize

Make notes in the second section of your outline on page 36.

Two Types of Igneous Rocks

The rate of cooling from liquid to solid helps scientists divide igneous rocks into two categories: extrusive and intrusive. **Extrusive igneous rocks** are formed when lava cools on the surface of the Earth. Since lava cools quickly, there is little time for crystals to form. For this reason extrusive igneous rocks have relatively small crystals.

The small crystal size of extrusive igneous rocks makes these rocks less valuable to humans. Although they can be crushed and processed as gravel for highways, most extrusive igneous rocks are mainly interesting additions to the landscape.

The counterparts to extrusive igneous rocks

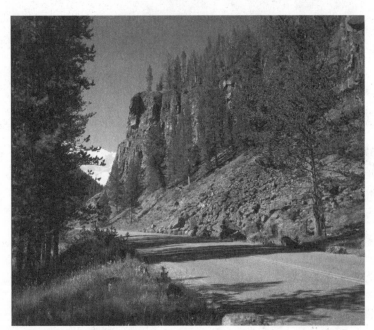

The Obsidian Cliffs in Yellowstone National Park are made of a type of glassy extrusive igneous rock called obsidian.

NAME ....

"Igneous Rocks"

are **intrusive igneous rocks.** Intrusive igneous rocks are formed when magma cools beneath the earth's surface. Many types of valuable metals such as iron, copper, and gold can be found in intrusive igneous rocks.

Like all igneous rocks, intrusive igneous rocks start out as magma. But the magma that solidifies into this type of rock begins cooling *before* it reaches the Earth's surface. The rate of cooling underground is slower than on the surface because other rocks act as blankets for the cooling rocks. This allows more time for crystal growth. As a result, the crystals in intrusive igneous rocks can be quite large. In many cases, the minerals found within these crystals are highly sought after.

Exotic minerals present in igneous rocks include amethysts, garnets, and zircons.

Stop and Organize

Make notes in the third section of your outline on page 36.

Plan

Now that you've previewed the science chapter, make a plan. Choose a strategy that can help you meet your reading purpose.

• An excellent strategy to use with science chapters is outlining.

Before you begin reading, create an Outline using the grid on page 36. Use the major headings in the chapter as the major headings in your Outline.

During Reading

D Read with a Purpose

Make notes on stickies as you read. Add the most important facts and details to your outline.

Directions: Now do a careful reading of the science chapter. Write your notes on this Outline.

Outline

I. The origin of igneous rocks

   A. Igneous rocks are formed from magma.

   B. Magma above ground is called lava.

II. The role of crystals

   A. Crystals are the building blocks of rock.

   B. Rock material that cools slowly produces large crystals.

   C. Rock material that cools quickly produces small crystals.

III. Two types of igneous rocks

   A. Extrusive igneous rocks are lava cooled on the surface of the Earth.

      1. They have small crystals.

      2. They are useful as gravel and for landscape detail.

   B. Intrusive igneous rocks are formed underneath Earth's surface.

      1. They have larger crystals.

      2. They may contain valuable metals and minerals.

         a. Iron, copper, and gold are examples of metals.

         b. Amethysts, garnets, and zircons are examples of minerals.

NAME ....

FOR USE WITH PAGES 88–99

Understanding How Science Texts Are Organized

Scientists often think in terms of cause and effect. Many science chapters are organized around this concept.

Directions: Reread the information about magma in the science chapter. Then complete the following organizer.

Cause-Effect Organizer

Effects

Cause

Hot magma formed under the Earth's surface begins rising above ground.

When the magma cools under the Earth's surface, it forms intrusive igneous rock.

When it cools above the surface, it forms extrusive igneous rock.

Textbooks

E Connect

As often as possible, make personal connections to a science chapter. These connections can help you remember what you've read.

• **You can connect to a science chapter by noting what the subject reminds you of from your own life.**

Directions: Reread this paragraph from the science chapter. Then, make some connection notes on the sticky.

The small crystal size of extrusive igneous rocks makes these rocks less valuable to humans. Although they can be crushed and processed as gravel for highways, most extrusive igneous rocks are mainly interesting additions to the landscape.

I've seen huge black stones in a few gardens in the suburbs. I wonder if these are extrusive igneous rocks? We've always called them "lava stones."

After Reading

When you finish a chapter, try to recall what you have learned. Use your outline to help you review.

F Pause and Reflect

Before moving on, stop and decide whether you've understood everything discussed in the science chapter.

• **Always return to your original reading purpose and see if you've accomplished what you set out to do.**

Directions: Answer these questions about the science chapter you just read.

Looking Back

Did I accomplish the reading purpose I set in the beginning? I think so.

Do I know what the main topics in the chapter are? Yes.

In my Outline, can I support each main topic with subtopics? Yes.

Would I feel comfortable taking a test on this material now? I'm not sure.

 Reread

It's unlikely that you'll be able to absorb every fact and detail with just one reading. Plan on rereading at least part of every chapter.

- **A powerful rereading strategy to use is note-taking.**

Directions: Make notes about key terms from the chapter on these study cards.

Study Cards

1. magma

2. lava

1. intrusive igneous rocks

2. extrusive igneous rocks

1. Magma is molten rock beneath the surface of the Earth. Magma hardens into solid rock as it cools.

2. Lava is molten rock that comes out of an erupting volcano. Lava hardens into solid rock as it cools.

1. Intrusive igneous rocks are rocks formed from magma under the surface of the Earth.

2. Extrusive igneous rock are rocks formed from lava on the surface of the Earth.

NAME

 H **Remember**

Good readers remember what they've read. Creating a practice test can help.

• **Testing yourself will help you remember the most important parts of a science chapter.**

Directions: Write sample test questions. Then, exchange books with a partner and have your partner answer them.

◂ **Practice Test**

Name of Partner

1. Question: What is the difference between extrusive and intrusive igneous rocks?

Answer: Intrusive igneous rocks are formed underground. Extrusive igneous rocks are formed when lava cools above ground.

2. Question: What are the names of the three classes of rocks?

Answer: igneous, sedimentary, and metamorphic

3. Question: What factor determines the size of the crystals formed in igneous rocks?

Answer: the rate of cooling

4. Question: What are two metals that can be found in intrusive igneous rocks?

Answer: gold and copper

Textbooks

Reading Math

To succeed in math, you must know how to read carefully, think critically, and apply what you've learned. Practice using the reading process with a math chapter here.

Before Reading

In math, one concept builds on another like rungs on a ladder. If you skip a rung, you're heading for trouble.

 ### A Set a Purpose

In most cases, you can set your purpose by turning the title of the chapter into questions.

> • **To set your purpose, ask one or more questions about the title of the chapter.**

<u>Directions:</u> On the lines below, write your purpose for reading a math chapter called "Solving Addition Equations."

Purpose question #1 *What are addition equations?*

Purpose question #2 *How do I solve an addition equation?*

B Preview

It's vitally important that you preview a math chapter. This will help you recall what you already know about the subject.

<u>Directions:</u> Preview the math chapter that follows. Make notes on the preview chart on the next page. You will fill in the third column later.

Preview Chart

What I Already Know	What I Need to Learn	What I Learned
I know that a variable is "the unknown." I know that you use subtraction to add negative numbers to positive numbers.	What is an addition equation? How do I solve this type of equation? How will I use this skill in real life?	An addition equation is a mathematical statement that is solved through the use of addition. To solve an addition equation, subtract the same number from both sides of the equation so that the variable is alone. Then, solve for the variable.

Chapter

6.1 Solving Addition Equations

Goals
- Learn how to solve addition equations.
- Understand how to use addition equations to solve real-life problems.

Key Terms
addition equation
variable

Goal 1 Solving addition equations

An addition equation is a mathematical statement that is solved through the use of addition. To solve an addition equation, subtract the same number from both sides of the equation so that the variable will be by itself on one side of the equation.

✔ Study Tip
Use mental math to solve addition equations when you can. But be sure you also know how to solve them step-by-step on paper.

Example 1 Solve this addition equation.

$x + 7 = -4$

Solution

$x + 7 = -4$ Original equation

$\underline{ -7 \quad -7}$ First, subtract 7 from both sides of the equation

$x = -11$ Solution

The solution is –11. You can check your answer this way:

Check:

$x + 7 = -4$ Original equation

$-11 + 7 = -4$ Substitute –11 for x

$-4 = -4$ Both sides are the same

Example 2 Solve the addition equation.

$$4 = n + 8$$

Solution

$4 = n + 8$	Original equation
$-8 \quad -8$	Subtract 8 from both sides of the equation
$-4 = n$	Solution

The solution is –4. Check your solution by returning to the original equation.

Goal 2 Solving Addition Equations in Real Life

Knowing how to solve addition equations can help you solve real-life problems that involve increases and decreases. For example, you use an addition equation if you want to find out how much the outdoor temperature has changed from one day to the next.

Example 3 On a Tuesday in March, the high temperature for the day was 3°. By Friday, the temperature rose to 27°. How many degrees did the temperature climb from Tuesday to Friday?

Solution

The way to solve this problem is to create an addition equation. Let t represent the unknown temperature.

$t + 3° = 27°$	Original equation
$-3° \quad -3°$	First, subtract –3° from both sides of the equation.
$t \quad = 24°$	Solution

The solution is 24°. This means that the temperature climbed 24° between Tuesday and Friday.

Double-check ✔✔ **Apply What You've Learned**

    a. $k + 7 = -3$ **b.** $3 = \partial + 6$

    c. $z + -9 = 46$ **d.** $11 = l + -8$

e. On the first week of the month, Julianne had $17 in her backpack. At the end of the month, she owed her friend Sue $7. How much did Julianne spend over the course of the month?

List the four steps for solving an addition equation.

1. Subtract the same number from both sides of the equation.

2. Check that the variable is by itself on one side of the equation.

3. Solve for the variable.

4. Check your work.

How does this subject apply to real life?

Knowing how to solve addition equations can help you solve real-life problems that involve increases and decreases.

Plan

After you preview, make a plan for reading. Use the strategy of visualizing and listing the steps you will need to learn to help you get *more* from a math chapter.

> • **Visualizing and thinking aloud helps you take an abstract idea (the math problem) and turn it into a concrete drawing or explanation.**

During Reading

 Read with a Purpose

Remember that your purpose for reading is to learn the skills taught in the chapter.

__Directions:__ Now do a careful reading of the sample math chapter. Make notes on the stickies.

Using the Strategy

Visualizing means drawing a diagram or sketch of the problem. Listing the steps will break down your task to its simplest parts.

__Directions:__ Reread the practice problem from the math chapter. Draw a sketch and then write down all the things you will have to do to solve it.

Sample Problem

On the first week of the month, Julianne had $17 in her backpack. At the end of the month, she owed her friend Sue $7. How much did Julianne spend over the course of the month?

Visualizing

Listing the Steps

1. I'd set up an addition equation that looks like this: $17 - x = -7$

2. I'd add the same number (7) to both sides of the equation.

3. I'd check to see that the variable is by itself on one side of the equation.

4. Then, I'd solve for the variable and check my work.

Understanding How Math Textbooks Are Organized

Most chapters in math textbooks open with a study guide or goals box that lists key terms and objectives. For example:

Goals
- Learn how to solve addition equations.
- Understand how to use addition equations to solve real-life problems.

Key Terms
addition equation
variable

After you finish your careful reading of the chapter, return to the study guide on the opening page. Be sure you've met each goal and learned each term.

Directions: Answer these questions using the notes you made while reading the math text.

What is an addition equation? An addition equation is a mathematical statement that is solved through the use of addition.

What is a variable? A variable is a letter used to represent a number value in an equation.

How do you solve an addition equation? To solve an addition equation, subtract the same number from both sides of the equation so that the variable will be by itself on one side of the equation.

How might you use an addition equation to solve a real-life problem? Knowing how to solve addition equations could help me solve real-life problems that involve increases and decreases.

NAME _____

 Connect

Math will feel more relevant to your life if you turn abstract problems into real-life ones.

- **Making a connection between a math problem and the real world can make the problem easier to solve.**

Directions: Review the chart at the top of page 109 in the *Reader's Handbook*. Then, write a real-life problem for the abstract problem in the chart below.

Real-life Problem

Abstract Problem	Real-life Problem
$700 + x = -300$	A player on a game show has $700 in the bank. In the final round she misses a question and ends up with -300. How much did she gain or lose with that final question?

After Reading

Always take a moment to think about what you've learned.

 Pause and Reflect

Return to your reading purpose. Ask yourself, "Have I met my purpose?" and "Did I learn what this chapter was trying to teach me?"

- **After you finish reading, ask yourself, "How well did I meet my purpose?"**

Directions: Answer these questions about the addition equations chapter.

Looking Back

Do I understand the key terms? Yes.
Do I know how to solve an addition equation? Yes.
Are the sample problems clear to me? Yes.
Can I complete the exercises? I think so.
Would I do well on a test that covered this material? I'm not sure.

Textbooks

Reread

Think about key strategies you learned from the chapter. If you don't understand one of them, you'll need to do some reviewing.

• **Use the rereading strategy of note-taking to help you remember information in the chapter.**

Directions: Read the concepts in the left-hand column. Write your own example of the concept in the right-hand column.

Key Word Notes

Key Words and Concepts	Examples
equation	$n + 50 = 75$ ($n + 50$ must have the same value as 75)
variable	Some examples are x, n, l, and so on. Variables are written in lowercase and usually are italicized.
addition equation	$4 + x = -19$
subtracting the same number	$-4 \qquad -4$
from both sides of the equation	$x = -23$

 Remember

Keep in mind that math concepts build on each other. Don't leave a chapter until you're certain you'll remember what you've learned.

• **A practice test can help you remember the important parts of a reading.**

Directions: Write a practice test on solving addition equations. Then, write the answer key.

Practice Test

Solve these addition equations.

a. $k + 7 = -3$ b. $3 = d + 6$

c. $z + -9 = 46$ d. $11 = l + -8$

Answer Key

a. -10 b. -3 c. 55 d. 19

Focus on Foreign Language

Reading a foreign language text is not that much different from reading a science or history text. The same reading process and reading tools apply.

Step 1 Read the paragraph.

Begin with an active reading of the textbook page. Make notes as you go.

Directions: Read the following page from a Spanish text. Make notes on the sticky.

Comparativos y Superlativos

Objectives

Understand how comparisons are made in Spanish.

➤➤Most of the adjectives you have learned so far can be used to compare things or people in this way:
El hombre es importante.
El hombre es más importante que el alcalde.

➤➤To say that something or someone is the "most" or "best," use *de* or *del*:
El hombre es la persona más importante de la ciudad.
Mi pueblo es lo más bonito del mundo.

NOTA

Use *de* when the object is feminine and *del* when the object is masculine. Remember that *lo* means "the one who" or "the one that" and describes the subject.

Ejercicios
El modelo
Lila es fuerte. (Yo)
Yo soy más fuerte que Lila.

Cambie las frases según el modelo.
1. El perro blanco es gordo. (flaco)
2. Guillermo es buen médico. (mal)
3. Señora Diego es buena cocinera. (la mejor)

What is the textbook page about?

Using the comparative and superlative forms of adjectives in Spanish

Step 2 Organize what you've learned.

Next, make a quick organizer to show what you've learned. This will help you process and remember the information.

Directions: Record your notes from the reading in this Web.

Web

Step 3 Commit what you've learned to memory.

Memorizing what you've read is an important part of learning a foreign language. Creating a study test can help.

Directions: Read the review tips on page 117 of the *Reader's Handbook*. Then write four test questions for the Spanish page you read.

Sample Test

1. How would you say, "She is the best student in the school"?

2. Translate "Fish is much better than chicken" into Spanish.

3. What is the difference between comparativo and superlativo?

4. Write "Téa is taller than Adele" in Spanish.

Focus on Science Concepts

Much of what you read in a science text will involve concepts. The reading process can help you master the information and techniques.

Step 1 Learn key terms.

To understand a science concept, you must first learn the key terms.

Directions: Look at the rock cycle diagram below. Write key words in the word bank on page 50. Then, use a dictionary to define each term.

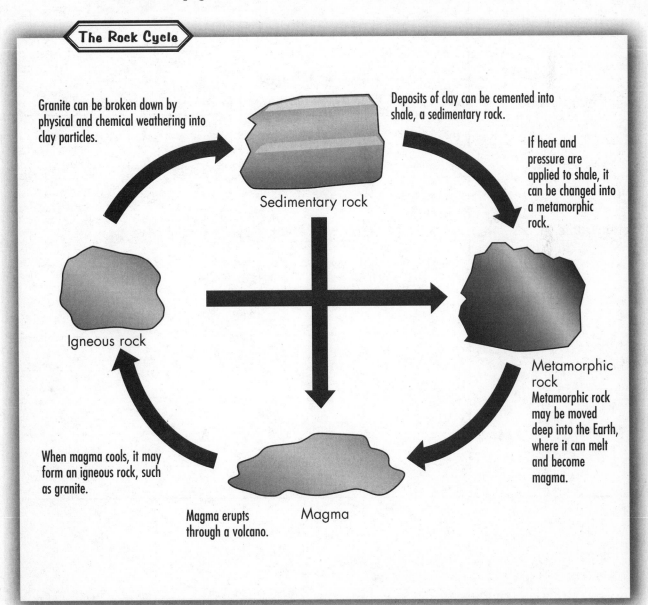

The Rock Cycle

Granite can be broken down by physical and chemical weathering into clay particles.

Deposits of clay can be cemented into shale, a sedimentary rock.

Sedimentary rock

If heat and pressure are applied to shale, it can be changed into a metamorphic rock.

Igneous rock

Metamorphic rock
Metamorphic rock may be moved deep into the Earth, where it can melt and become magma.

When magma cools, it may form an igneous rock, such as granite.

Magma erupts through a volcano.

Magma

Word Bank

Word	Definition
igneous rocks	Rocks formed from lava or magma.
weathering	The breaking up of rocks on the Earth's surface by rain, ice, and changes in temperature
erosion	The gradual wearing away of soil and rock from the Earth's surface
sedimentary rocks	Rocks that form from clay particles cemented together or from evaporating water or from buried remnants of animals or from plants that have been heated and compressed under the ground
metamorphic rocks	A kind of rock formed when another rock is changed by the heat and/or pressure in the Earth's crust
magma	Molten rock beneath the surface of the Earth

Step 2 Track steps in the process.

Now, figure out how the process works.

Directions: Write the steps of the rock cycle here. Use key terms from your word bank.

Flow Chart

Magma erupts through a volcano as lava and cools into igneous rocks.

▼

Weathering and erosion wear away at the igneous rocks.

▼

The weathered rocks are reduced to clay.

▼

The clay becomes sedimentary rocks.

▼

Sedimentary rocks are transformed into metamorphic rocks through heat and pressure.

▼

Metamorphic rocks melt and become magma.

Textbooks

Step 3 Retell the process.

Finish by describing the process to a friend. This will help you retain what you've learned.

Directions: Retell the steps in the rock cycle on the lines below. Refer to your notes as needed.

Retelling

First, magma erupts through a volcano. At this point the magma is called lava. The lava hardens into igneous rocks. Weathering and erosion wear away the igneous rocks over time. Eventually, the weathered rock is reduced to clay. The clay becomes sedimentary rocks, which in turn are transformed into metamorphic rocks with additional heat and pressure. Metamorphic rocks may change from a solid to a liquid and become magma. This step brings the cycle full circle.

Focus on Study Questions

Reading a question carefully is an important first step in answering it. Careful readers know that most questions require two or even three readings.

Step 1 Read the question two times or more.

Begin by reading the question at least twice. Find the key words.

Directions: Read this sample question. Highlight the key words.

> **Sample Question**
>
> Summarize the Supreme Court's ruling in *Plessy* v. *Ferguson*. Then, explain the effect it had on African-American children in the South.

Step 2 Choose a strategy.

Next, choose a strategy that can help you answer the question. In many cases, visualizing and thinking aloud will be your best choices.

Directions: On the lines below, explain what you need to do to answer the *Plessy* v. *Ferguson* question. Then, name the strategy you'll use.

To answer the question, I will need to describe what was involved in Plessy v. Ferguson and

then explain the effect the ruling had on southern African-American children.

Strategy I'll use: thinking aloud because I need to talk through my answer before I begin

writing.

Step 3 Answer the question.

Next, use the strategy to answer the question.

Directions: Write a Think Aloud for the *Plessy* v. *Ferguson* question.

◀ Think Aloud

Partner:

The first thing I need to do is explain the Plessy v. Ferguson decision. I'll give some basic facts about the decision, like dates, parties involved, and something that includes the "separate but equal" quote from the ruling. Then, I'll talk about how African-American children in the South were forced to go to inferior schools that most often provided inferior educations. Many Southerners believed that the Plessy v. Ferguson ruling sanctioned the Jim Crow laws that they had been enforcing for years.

Step 4 Check your answer.

The last step is to check your work. Reread the question and then ask yourself, "Is my answer reasonable?"

Directions: Reread your answer. Exchange books with a partner. Read your partner's writing and make comments in the margin. Check to be sure that your partner's answer is reasonable.

NAME ....

Focus on Word Problems

Have you noticed that the word problems in math class seem to be getting trickier and trickier? But even the hardest problems are solved in basically the same way. Using a four-step reading plan will help eliminate the confusion.

Step 1 Read the problem.

The first step in solving a word problem is to read it carefully.

Directions: Read the following word problem. Highlight key words. Make notes on the sticky.

> ◆ **Sample Question**
>
> The daily noontime temperature in Detroit during the first week of March was 5° F. On Saturday and Sunday, the noontime temperature dropped to –5°F. What was the average daily noontime temperature for that first week in March? Round to the nearest degree.

The topic is: noontime temperatures during a week in March

The given is: The temperature was 5°F during the week and -5°F on the weekend.

I need to find: the average daily noontime temperature for the week.

Step 2 Choose a strategy.

The best strategy to use with word problems is visualizing and thinking aloud.

Directions: Make a sketch that shows the daily temperature problem.

◆ **Sketch**

x 5 days

x 2 days

Step 3 Solve.

Use your strategy to solve the problem.

Directions: Write a numerical expression for the problem. Then solve it.

$[(5° \times 5) + (-5° \times 2)] \div 7 = T$

$[25° + -10°] \div 7 = T$

$15° \div 7 = 2.14$

$T = 2°F$

Step 4 Check.

Your last step is to check your work. Is your answer reasonable?

Directions: Write a Think Aloud that shows how you solved the problem.

Think Aloud

To find the average daily temperature for the week, I first had to add the 5 weekday temperatures to get 25°. Then I added the 2 weekend temperatures to get -10°. Next, I added the two numbers together and got 15°. I divided this number by 7 to find the average temperature for the 7 days. Then, I rounded my answer (2.14°) to the nearest degree and ended up with an average daily temperature of 2°.

Reading a Personal Essay

A personal essay is informal and can deal with any subject. In most personal essays, the writer opens with an interesting autobiographical story. Later in the essay, the writer explains a point, insight, or lesson that can be taken from that story.

Before Reading

Practice reading and responding to a personal essay here. Use the reading process and the strategy of outlining to help you read an essay by Max Beerbohm.

 A Set a Purpose

Your purpose will be to find the subject and main idea of the essay. In addition, you'll want to decide how you feel about the essayist's main idea.

- **To set your purpose, ask questions about the essay's subject and main idea.**

Directions: Write three purpose questions for the essay "Going Out for a Walk."

Purpose question 1: What is the subject of "Going Out for a Walk"?

Purpose question 2: What is the main idea of the essay?

Purpose question 3: How do I feel about the main idea?

 B Preview

Always preview an essay before you begin reading. Pay careful attention to these key parts:

Preview Checklist

- ☑ the title and author
- ☑ the first and last paragraphs
- ☑ any repeated words or phrases
- ☑ any key words or words in boldface or italics

Nonfiction

Directions: Preview "Going Out for a Walk." Write your preview notes on this Web. Add more boxes if you need to.

Web

Author's name:

Max Beerbohm

Essay subject:

Something about taking a walk

Repeated words:

walk, I, walking, friend, place, definite, never

"Going Out for a Walk"

Background information:

Max Beerbohm was a famous essayist. He liked to poke fun at pretentious or absurd people and things in British society.

First paragraph details:

The essayist himself never voluntarily goes out for a walk. Sometimes he's dragged out on a walk, but he would never initiate this activity on his own.

Last paragraph details:

It turns out that he composed the essay in his head during a walk, which seems funny. But I see that he's still saying that he will never go for a walk.

from "Going Out for a Walk" by Max Beerbohm

Max Beerbohm (1872-1956) was a British essayist who was famous for his witty criticism of anything that was pretentious or absurd in English society. In this essay, which was published in 1919, Beerbohm pokes fun at men and women who go out walking when they have absolutely nowhere to go.

It is a fact that not once in all my life have I gone out for a walk. I have been taken out for walks; but that is another matter. Even while I trotted prattling by my nurse's side I regretted the good old days when I had, and wasn't, a perambulator. When I grew up it seemed to me that the one advantage of living in London was that nobody ever wanted me to come out for a walk. London's very drawbacks—its endless noise and hustle, its smoky air, the squalor ambushed everywhere in it—assured this one immunity. Whenever I was with friends in the country, I knew that at any moment, unless rain were actually falling, some man might suddenly say "Come out for a walk!" in that sharp imperative tone which he would not dream of using in any other connection.

Stop and Organize
Make some notes in the "Introduction" section of your Outline on page 61.

People seem to think there is something inherently noble and virtuous in the desire to go for a walk. Anyone thus desirous feels that he has a right to impose his will on whomever he sees comfortably settled in an arm-chair, reading. It is easy to say simply "No" to an old friend. In the case of a mere acquaintance one wants some excuse. "I wish I could, but"—nothing ever occurs to me except "I have some letters to write." This formula is unsatisfactory in three ways. (1) It isn't believed. (2) It compels you to rise from your chair, go to the writing-table, and sit improvising a letter to somebody until the walkmonger (just not daring to call you liar and hypocrite) shall have lumbered out of the room. (3) It won't operate on Sunday mornings. "There's no post out till this evening" clinches the matter; and you may as well go quietly.

Stop and Organize
Make some notes in the "Body" section of your Outline on page 61.

Walking for walking's sake may be as highly laudable and exemplary a thing as it is held to be by those who practice it. My objection to it is that it stops the brain.

Nonfiction

from "Going Out for a Walk" by Max Beerbohm

Many a man has professed to me that his brain never works so well as when he is swinging along the high road or over hill and dale. This boast is not confirmed by my memory of anybody who on a Sunday morning has forced me to partake of his adventure. Experience teaches me that whatever a fellow-guest may have of power to instruct or to amuse when he is sitting on a chair, or standing on a hearth-rug, quickly leaves him when he takes one out for a walk. The ideas that came so thick and fast to him in any room, where are they now? where that encyclopaedic knowledge which he bore so lightly? where the kindling fancy that played like summer lightning over any topic that was started? The man's face that was so mobile is set now; gone is the light from his fine eyes. He says that A. (our host) is a thoroughly good fellow. Fifty yards further on, he adds that A. is one of the best fellows he has ever met. We tramp another furlong or so, and he says that Mrs. A. is a charming woman. Presently he adds that she is one of the most charming women he has ever known. We pass an inn. He reads vapidly aloud to me: "The King's Arms. Licensed to sell Ales and Spirits." I foresee that during the rest of the walk he will read aloud any inscription that occurs. We pass a milestone. He points at it with his stick, and says "Uxminster. 11 Miles." We turn a sharp corner at the foot of a hill. He points at the wall, and says "Drive Slowly." I see far ahead, on the other side of the hedge bordering the high road, a small notice-board. He sees it too. He keeps his eye on it. And in due course "Trespassers," he says, "Will Be Prosecuted." Poor man!—mentally a wreck. . . .

Stop and Organize
Make some more notes in the "Body" section of your Outline on page 61.

. . . Such as it is, this essay was composed in the course of a walk, this morning. I am not one of those extremists who must have a vehicle to every destination. I never go out of my way, as it were, to avoid exercise. I take it as it comes, and take it in good part. That valetudinarians[1] are always chattering about it, and indulging in it to excess, is no reason for despising it. I am inclined to think that in moderation it is rather good for one, physically. But, pending a time when no people wish me to go and see them, and I have no wish to go and see anyone, and there is nothing whatever for me to do off my own premises, I never will go out for a walk.

Stop and Organize
Make some notes in the "Conclusion" section of you Outline on page 61.

1. **valetudinarians**—sickly persons

C Plan

Now, make a reading plan that will help you meet your purpose. Many readers find that the strategy of outlining can help you get *more* from an essay.

• **Outlining forces you to decide what information is the most important in an essay.**

During Reading

Watch for the three major parts of the essay: the introduction, the body, and the conclusion. If you need help with these terms, see page 159 of the *Reader's Handbook.*

D Read with a Purpose

Keep your purpose questions in mind as you read. Remember that you are looking for the topic and main idea of the essay.

Directions: Do a careful reading of "Going Out for a Walk." Make notes on this Outline as you read.

Outline

I. Introduction

A. Detail: He hated walking as a baby.

B. Detail: He likes London because no one wants to walk.

C. Detail: In the country, however, walking seems to be "required."

II. Body

A. Detail: It's easy to say "no" when it's a friend inviting you for a walk.

B. Detail: It's impossible to think of a lie that will convince a would-be walker.

C. Detail: Walking stops the brain and makes lively, intelligent people seem like bores.

III. Conclusion

A. Detail: Walking may be fine for some people, but he will not walk aimlessly.

B. Detail: He composed the essay during a walk, but that's not the same.

C. Detail: He doesn't avoid exercise, but he doesn't seek it out, either.

Understanding How Essays Are Organized

Most personal essays are organized in a funnel pattern.

> • In a funnel pattern, the writer builds toward the main idea.

Directions: Complete this organizer with information from "Going Out for a Walk."

Name the topic here.   Going out for a walk

List details that relate to the topic here.

People make demands about it.

Lying to get out of it never works.

Walking stops the brain and makes people act like fools.

Write a key detail from the conclusion here.

He admits to composing the essay while walking, but he

was alone.

Write the essayist's main idea here.

Going for a walk is a dreadful

thing to do because

it turns people

into fools.

E Connect

Remember that part of your reading purpose involves deciding how you feel about the essayist's main idea.

> • Connect to an essay by recording your thoughts and feelings about the main idea.

Directions: Read this sentence from the essay. Write your reaction to it on the sticky.

But, pending a time when no people wish me to go and see them, and I have no wish to go and see anyone, and there is nothing whatever for me to do off my own premises, I never will go out for a walk.

He sounds like an old crank here, but I think he is kind of funny. He makes such a big deal about going for a walk! But it's the stuff that goes along with the walking that bugs him the most.

After Reading

When you finish reading, take a moment or two to think about what the author has said.

F Pause and Reflect

Ask yourself questions about the essay and your purpose for reading.

- **After you finish an essay, ask yourself, "How well did I meet my purpose?"**

Directions: Answer these questions about "Going Out for a Walk."

Looking Back

What is the subject of the essay? *The subject is going for a walk.*

What does the author say about the subject? *It's a dreadful thing to do because it turns people into foolish bores.*

How do you feel about the author's message? *I think it's funny. But I'm intolerant of fools and bores, too. I see them everywhere, not only when I'm walking!*

Do you feel you've met your reading purpose? *I think I have, but I need to double-check that I've gotten the main idea exactly right.*

G Reread

The strategy of questioning the author can help you if you're not sure you've fully understood the essay.

- **A powerful rereading strategy to use is questioning the author.**

Nonfiction

Directions: Write three questions that you would like to ask Max Beerbohm. Then, write the answers you think he might have given.

Questioning the Author

Question 1: What is your message in the essay?

_____

Beerbohm's answer: I wanted to make fun of people who go for walks for no real reason other

than because it is "what everybody does."

Question 2: Why do you mention that you composed the essay while walking?

_____

Beerbohm's answer: Well, I wanted to show that I understand walking if there's some purpose

involved. Also, I wanted to sort of surprise the readers, so that they remember the essay.

Question 3: What is your tone in the essay?

_____

Beerbohm's answer: Humorous and critical at the same time

_____

 H **Remember**

Completing an organizer can help you remember what you've just read.

- **A Main Idea Organizer can help you pull together everything you've learned.**

Directions: Complete this organizer using notes from your reading.

Main Idea Organizer

Topic: Going for a walk		
Main Idea: It's a dreadful thing to do because it makes fools out of people.		
Detail 1	**Detail 2**	**Detail 3**
"Walkmongers" are fanatical in their insistence that you come for a walk.	They say stupid things.	They become terribly boring.

Reading an Editorial

The purpose of most editorials is to advance an argument or comment on the important issues of the day. Your job as the reader is to understand and evaluate the assertions the writer makes.

Before Reading

Practice reading and responding to an editorial here. Employing the strategy of questioning the author will help you fully grasp the author's points.

A Set a Purpose

Your purpose is to understand the author's viewpoint, evaluate how persuasively the point is supported, and decide how you feel about it.

- **To set your purpose, ask questions about the viewpoint and support.**

Directions: Write your purpose for reading the editorial "A Modest Rebuttal" on the lines below.

Purpose question #1 What is the writer's modest rebuttal?

Purpose question #2 How does the writer support that viewpoint?

Purpose question #3 What is my opinion of what the author is saying?

B Preview

Your main goal when previewing is to get a sense of the subject of the editorial. Take a close look at the items on this checklist:

Preview Checklist

- ☑ the headline and date
- ☑ any repeated words
- ☑ the first and last paragraphs
- ☑ the writer's assertion

Nonfiction

Directions: Preview "A Modest Rebuttal." Write your preview notes on the chart below. Then infer what you think is the topic of the editorial.

Preview Chart

Items Previewed	My Notes
the headline	"A Modest Rebuttal"
the date	January 17
the first paragraph	There is a debate raging in this school district.
the last paragraph	If they're given plenty of meal choices, teens will choose well.
repeated words and phrases	issue, debate, cafeteria, high school, junk food

I think the editorial is going to be about: whether teens are responsible enough to eat sensibly.

The Valley High School Times

Volume 42: Issue 14   January 17

A Modest Rebuttal

Every year, right around the beginning of September, school district officials, teachers, and parents stir themselves up into a frenzy of debate and handwringing. The issue that is riling our role models? Is it poverty in our cities or homelessness on our streets? Is it landfills filling, factories polluting, or eagles expiring?

Actually, it's none of these things. The issue that's causing all the wailing and worrying is a debate over junk food. To be more specific—it is whether or not junk food should be served in the high school cafeteria.

Stop and Organize
Why does the author begin this way? Make notes on your Double-entry Journal on page 69.

"A Modest Rebuttal"

To many, the question of whether our school should be allowed to "peddle" junk food is all but unanswerable. School nurses say no to burgers and fries; cafeteria workers say yes. Parents say no; kids say yes. It's the unending debate—or so it seems.

In reality, a little research can go a long way toward answering this question and resolving the debate. A quick reading of *The California Journal of Nutrition* or a few minutes' research on the Internet yields a wealth of nutritional data that even Betty Crocker could not dispute.

The fact of the matter is, serving junk food in the school cafeteria has little or no effect on the overall health of students and can actually *benefit* students by encouraging them to make healthier meal choices at other times during the day.

Stop and Organize

What point is the author making here? Make notes on your Double-entry Journal on page 69.

Last year, a group of local nutritionists, led by Dr. Dionne Landers of City Hospital, surveyed twelve different high schools in our state. All twelve of these schools had just recently begun serving junk food in their cafeterias.

Each school participating in the survey was asked to instruct students to keep a food journal of everything they ate for lunch and dinner in the month of September.

At the end of the month, Landers and her group began reading the students' food journals. "What we found in these journals surprised us very much," Dr. Landers reports. "We expected to learn that kids were choosing junk food five lunches a week, and then going home and eating basically the same thing for dinner."

Instead, Landers and her colleagues learned that the opposite was true. Their findings indicated that students who ate a junk food lunch tended to eat a well-balanced dinner. On the other hand, students who chose the cafeteria special—which by law must meet federal nutritional requirements for teens—tended to eat a "junky" dinner.

Stop and Organize

How does this information support the author's assertion? Make notes on your Double-entry Journal on page 69.

"Basically what we were seeing is that those students who ate burgers and fries for lunch would compensate by eating pasta and a salad for dinner. They did this either consciously or unconsciously. Students, however, who chose the cafeteria special for lunch tended to opt for burgers and fries for dinner."

After the survey was finished, Landers and her group published their report and filed it with the state department of education. What the report says, in essence, is that teens who are

"A Modest Rebuttal"

given plenty of choices end up meeting their daily nutritional requirement without even realizing it.

Critics of the plan to serve burgers, fries, and pizza in our school cafeteria should take a careful look at Landers's data. Their charge that malnutrition reigns where burger is king is clearly refuted in Landers's report.

The truth of the matter is that if they are given plenty of meal choices, most teens will choose well. So let us have a burger, fries, and soda at lunch, and then it's please pass the broccoli at dinner.

Stop and Organize

What action are readers supposed to take or how are readers supposed to feel as a result of this editorial? Make notes on your Double-entry Journal on page 69.

C Plan

After your preview, make a plan for reading. Choose a strategy that can help you take note of the author's assertions (statements about the topic) and the support for the assertions. An excellent strategy to use is questioning the author.

- **Use the strategy of questioning the author to help you find the writer's assertions and support.**

During Reading

D Read with a Purpose

Keep your purpose in mind as you read. Remember that you want to find out what point the author is making and how he or she supports that point. Asking (and answering) questions can help.

Directions: Do a careful reading of the editorial. Ask questions of the author. Make notes on the following Double-entry Journal.

Double-entry Journal

Questions	My Thoughts
Why does the author begin this way?	I think the author is being kind of sarcastic as a way of grabbing the reader's attention. The author wants to play up the opinion that adults in the district are making a big deal of a pretty stupid issue.
What point is the author making here?	If people would do a little research, they'd find out that serving junk food in the school cafeteria can benefit students by encouraging them to make healthier meal choices at other times during the day.
How does this information support the author's assertion?	Dr. Landers's data from the twelve schools shows students eating junk food for lunch and then eating nutritious food for dinner.
What action are readers supposed to take or how are readers supposed to feel as a result of this editorial?	The editorial is directed toward the district officials, teachers, and parents. They are named in the opening paragraph. The writer wants them to quit squabbling about the issue and give kids the right to choose junk food for lunch if they want to.

Nonfiction

Using the Strategy

After you ask and answer the questions, use a critical reading chart to evaluate the information in the editorial.

__Directions:__ Record your answers to these critical reading questions.

Critical Reading Chart

Questions	My Thoughts
1. What topic is the writer discussing?	The writer is discussing serving junk food in the school cafeteria.
2. How does the writer feel about the topic?	He or she seems to feel pretty strongly about it and is critical of those who oppose the junk-food idea.
3. What are the writer's assertions?	Junk food at lunch won't harm health of students. Junk food at lunch will cause students to make healthy eating decisions at other times during the day. Junk food should be served.
4. How does the writer support the assertions?	The writer has evidence from a report written by a nutritionist named Dr. Dionne Landers.
5. What do I think about this topic?	I think it's an interesting debate. My school went through this a couple of years ago. Now they serve junk food on some days.
6. How do my thoughts compare with those of the writer?	I agree. Students should be allowed to choose what they eat for lunch.

Understanding How Editorials Are Organized

Most editorials contain three parts: the writer's assertions, the support, and the recommendation. Very often the parts follow the structure like the one on page 175 of the *Reader's Handbook*.

- **Most editorials contain assertions, support for the assertions, and a recommendation.**

Directions: Record the writer's assertions, support, and recommendation in "A Modest Rebuttal" on this organizer.

Editorial Structure

1. Assertion Fast food at lunch won't be harmful.

Supporting detail Landers's study

▼

2. Assertion Fast food at lunch will cause students to make healthy eating decisions at other times during the day.

Supporting detail Data from Landers's food journals

▼

3. Recommendations Offer fast food as an option in the high school cafeteria.

E Connect

Connecting to an editorial is important and easy. You react to the author's assertions and compare them to your own experience. Deciding how you feel about the writer's argument is an important part of your reading purpose.

• **Connect to an editorial by recording your thoughts and feelings.**

Directions: Reread the final two paragraphs of the editorial. Then, make notes on the sticky.

Critics of the plan to serve burgers, fries, and pizza in our school cafeteria should take a careful look at Landers's data. Their charge that malnutrition reigns when burger is king is clearly refuted in Landers's report.

The truth of the matter is that if they are given plenty of meal choices, most teens will choose well. So let us have a burger, fries, and soda at lunch, and then it's please pass the broccoli at dinner.

I think it makes a lot of sense. The people in that district should study Dr. Landers's report. I know from my own experience that I can't eat junk all day—I just can't. Sometimes I too say "pass the broccoli."

After Reading

It's not a bad idea to spend a few minutes thinking about an editorial after you finish reading it. After all, you never know when the information you've learned will come in handy.

F Pause and Reflect

Ask yourself questions about the editorial and your purpose for reading.

• **After you finish an editorial, ask yourself, "Do I understand the author's ideas and opinions?"**

Directions: Answer these questions about "A Modest Rebuttal."

Questions

What is the "modest rebuttal"? *The writer is refuting the claim that junk food for lunch is bad for kids.*

Can you explain how the writer supports the viewpoint? *Yes. The author offers evidence that includes a study done by nutritionists.*

Do you know how you feel about the editorial? *Yes, I'm pretty clear on it. But I'd like to find out a few more facts about the survey that the nutritionists did.*

NAME

 G **Reread**

Sometimes you may feel you need to reread an editorial. Maybe you want to find out more about the author's viewpoint. Or maybe you'd like to take another look at the author's support for the viewpoint.

• **A powerful rereading strategy to use with an editorial is synthesizing.**

Synthesizing means examining bits of information from a piece of writing and then putting them together to see what they mean.

Directions: Complete this synthesizing chart. Use the notes you made while reading the editorial.

◄ **Synthesizing Chart**

Editorial	My Thoughts
Topic: junk food in the lunchroom at school	What's my opinion? I agree with the writer.
What are the author's assertions? Junk food at lunch won't harm health of students. Junk food at lunch will cause students to make healthy eating decisions at other times during the day. Junk food should be served in the high school lunchroom.	Supporting detail #1 My observations in my own cafeteria
	Supporting detail #2 My own experiences with too much junk food in a given day
Supporting detail #1 survey	
	Supporting detail #3 Comments from students who are not allowed to have junk food in the cafeteria
Supporting detail #2 food journals	
	My conclusion: You can trust teens to make their own food choices.

Nonfiction

H **Remember**

Good readers remember what they've read. Writing a letter to a friend can help lock the ideas in your head.

> • **Writing a letter can help you remember the most important points in an editorial.**

Directions: Write a brief letter to a friend. In your letter, explain the writer's point in "A Modest Rebuttal" and your opinion of it.

Letter

Janet,

I read this really great editorial in my cousin's school newspaper. It talks about some of the things kids are saying in our school. Basically, the point of the editorial was to convince teachers, district officials, and parents that it's OK to serve junk food in the lunchroom. The writer gave all kinds of support for the viewpoint and quoted nutritionists and everything else.

I totally agree with what the editorial says. The argument is rational and well supported. I'm going to make a copy and show it to our journalism teacher at school.

Reading a News Story

Reading a news story is like hunting for shells on the beach.
The facts are there, if you know how to find them. The
reading process can help.

Before Reading

Here, you'll use the reading process to help you read and understand a news
story that was published in 1919.

A Set a Purpose

Begin by setting your purpose. In most cases, your purpose will be to find
out answers to these questions: *who, what, where, when, why,* and *how.*

- **To set your purpose, ask *who, what, where, when, why,* and *how***
  questions about the story's headline.

<u>Directions:</u> Write your purpose for reading "Ghastly Deeds of Race Rioters
Told" on the lines below. Then, explain what you already know about
the subject.

My purpose question: *What were the ghastly deeds of the race rioters?*

This is what I know about the subject: *I know these riots occurred well before the Civil Rights movement, so I can imagine how horrible they were. At the time, most African Americans were very poor. Their children were not well educated, and the government ignored their pleas for help. I'm sure that these and other factors contributed to the violence.*

B Preview

Use your preview time to get a handle on the topic of the article. Pay
attention to items on this checklist.

> **Preview Checklist**

☑ the headline

☑ the lead

☑ any key words or repeated phrases

Nonfiction

Directions: Preview the background information and lead of "Ghastly Deeds of Race Rioters Told." Make notes on this 5 W's and H Organizer.

5 W's and H Organizer

Who	What	Where	When	Why	How
whites and African Americans	horrible, bloody riots	Chicago	July 1919	racial prejudice	murder, arson, looting

In the spring and summer of 1919, bloody race riots erupted in 22 American cities and towns. The most severe of these took place in Chicago, in late July. The violence began when white beachgoers attacked several black youths who had drifted toward one of the "Whites Only" Lake Michigan beaches. Five days of intense racial violence followed in many parts of the city. A total of 23 African-American and 15 white Chicagoans were killed. More than 500 whites and blacks were badly injured, and thousands were burned out of their homes. The article that follows was written by a reporter for the Chicago Defender. It was published on the fifth and final day of the riots.

Ghastly Deeds of Race Rioters Told

For fully four days this old city has been rocked in a quake of racial antagonism, seared in a blaze of red hate flaming as fiercely as the heat of day— each hour ushering in new stories of slaying, looting, arson, and rape, sending the awful roll of casualties to a grand total of 40 dead and more than 500 wounded, many of them perhaps fatally. A certain madness distinctly indicated in reports of shootings, stabbings, and burning of buildings which literally pour in every minute. Women and children have not been spared. Traffic has been stopped. Phone wires have been cut.

Stores and Offices Shut

Victims lay in every street and vacant lot. Hospitals are filled: 4,000 troops rest in arms, among which are companies of the old Eighth regiment, while the inadequate force of police battles vainly to save the city's honor.

"Ghastly Deeds of Race Rioters Told"

Fear to Care for Bodies

Undertakers on the South Side refused to accept the bodies of white victims. White undertakers refused to accept black victims. Both for the same reason. They feared the vengeance of the mobs without.

Every little while bodies were found in some street, alley, or vacant lot—and no one sought to care for them. Patrols were unable to accommodate them because they were being used in rushing live victims to hospitals. Some victims were dragged to a mob's "No Man's Land" and dropped.

The telephone wires in the raging districts were cut in many places by the rioters, as it became difficult to estimate the number of dead victims. . . .

Monday Sees "Reign of Terror"

Following the Sunday affray, the red tongues had blabbed their fill, and Monday morning found the thoroughfares in the white neighborhoods throated with a sea of humans—everywhere—some armed with guns, bricks, clubs, and an oath. The presence of a black face in their vicinity was a signal for a carnival of death, and before any aid could reach the poor, unfortunate one his body reposed in some kindly gutter, his brains spilled over a dirty pavement. Some of the victims were chased, caught, and dragged into alleys and lots, where they were left for dead. In all parts of the city, white mobs dragged from surface cars, black passengers wholly ignorant of any

trouble, and set upon them. An unidentified man, young woman, and a 3-month old baby were found dead on the street at the intersection of 47th Street and Wentworth Avenue. She had attempted to board a car there when the mob seized her, beat her, slashed her body into ribbons, and beat the baby's brains out against a telegraph pole. . . . All the time this was happening, several policemen were in the crowd, but did not make any attempt to make rescue until too late.

Stop and Record
What facts does the reporter give? What opinions does he give? Record them on your Critical Reading Chart on page 80.

Kill Scores Coming from Yards

Rioters operating in the vicinity of the stockyards, which lies in the heart of white residences west of Halsted Street, attacked scores of workers—women and men alike returning from work. Stories of these outrages began to flutter into the black vicinities and hysterical men harangued their fellows to avenge the killings—and soon they, infected with the insanity of the mob, rushed through the streets, drove high powered motorcars, or waited for streetcars which they attacked with gunfire and stones. Shortly after noon all traffic south of 22nd Street and north of 55th Street, west of Cottage Grove Avenue and east of Wentworth Avenue, was stopped with the exception

Nonfiction

NAME ....

FOR USE WITH PAGES 181–192

"Ghastly Deeds of Race Rioters Told"

of trolley cars. Whites who entered this zone were set upon with unmeasurable fury.

Policemen employed in the disturbed sections were wholly unable to handle the situation. When one did attempt to carry out his duty he was beaten and his gun taken from him. The fury of the mob could not be abated. Mounted police were employed, but to no avail.

35th Vortex of Night's Rioting

With the approach of darkness the rioting gave prospects of being continued throughout the night. Whites boarded the platforms and shot through the windows of the trains at passengers. Some of the passengers alighting themselves from cars were thrown from the elevated structure, suffering broken legs, fractured skulls, and death.

The block between State Street and Wabash Avenue on East 35th Street was the scene of probably the most shooting and rioting of the evening and a pitched battle ensued between the police, whites, and blacks.

The trouble climaxed when white occupants of the Angelus apartments began firing shots and throwing missiles from their windows. One man was shot through the head, but before his name could be secured he was spirited away. The attack developed a hysterical battling fervor and the mob charged the building and the battle was on.

Police were shot. Whites were seen to tumble out of automobiles, from doorways, and other places, wounded or suffering from bruises inflicted by gunshots, stones, or bricks. A reign of terror literally ensued. Automobiles were stopped, occupants beaten, and machines wrecked. Streetcars operating in 35th Street were wrecked as well as north and south bound State Street cars. Windows were shattered and white occupants beaten. . . .

Stores Looted: Homes Burned

Tiring of street fights, rioters turned to burning and looting. This was truly a sleepless night and a résumé of the day's happenings nourished an inclination for renewed hostilities from another angle. The homes of blacks isolated in white neighborhoods were burned to the ground and the owners and occupants beaten and thrown unconscious in the smoldering embers. Meanwhile rioters in the "black belt" smashed windows and looted the shops of white merchants on State Street.

Other rioters, manning high powered cars and armed, flitted up and down the darkened streets, chancing shots at fleeing whites on the street and those riding in streetcars.

Toward midnight quiet reigned along State Street under the vigilance of 400 policemen and scores of uniformed men of the 8th Regiment.

Stop and Record

How does the reporter feel about the riots? Make notes in the main idea section of your Critical Reading Chart on page 80.

"Ghastly Deeds of Race Rioters Told"

Rioting Extends Into Loop

Tuesday dawned sorrowing with a death toll of 20 dead and 300 injured. . . . But hell was yet to break loose, and by fate I was destined to be present. It occurred at Wabash Avenue and 35th Street at 8:10 o'clock at night, when over fifty policemen, mounted and on foot, while in the attempt to disperse a mob that was playing havoc with every white face, drew their revolvers and showered bullets into the crowd. The officers' guns barked for fully ten minutes. Seeing no way to escape and at the same time thinking of the obituary column, I immediately decided that my best move was to fall face downward to the pavement and remain there 'til the air cleared. This I did at the expense of a perfectly new straw bonnet. But it was worth it.

Stop and Record

Are the reporter's sources authoritative and reliable? Make notes on your Critical Reading Chart on page 80.

Four Wounded

During the reign of terror four citizens fell wounded; one a woman. She voiced her distress after a bullet had pierced her left shoulder. A man of slender proportions stumbled over my body in the hurried attempt to escape and plunged head first into the ground. A stream of blood gushed from a wound in the back of his neck. The bullet from an officer's revolver had found its mark. Blood from his fatal wound trickled down the pavement until it had reached me and heated corpuscles bathed my left cheek as I awaited the cessation of hostilities. The pavement about me was literally covered with splintered glass which had been torn from a laundry window by the fusillade of shots, and several times I was tempted to brush the broken fragments from my back, where some had fallen, but I dreaded making a move. I had a reason. It was a case of eventuality, but not now.

Beads of perspiration rolled off my forehead as a bullet passed over the back of my coat, burning a path near the collar as it sped on its deathly mission. I arose reluctantly as a cop yelled: "Get up, everybody." He said it in the 200-point type we use on the front page of extras. His command was obeyed.

The wounded were whisked away in automobiles to nearby hospitals for treatment. Shortly after the guns had ceased firing the telephone on the managing editor's desk at the office tinkled. He answered.

"Have you heard of the shooting at 35th and Wabash Avenue?" queried a mellow tone voice on the other end. The rejoinder came, evidenced in clear tones: "Yes, madam, a *Defender* reporter was passing."

Nonfiction

Plan

Now that you have a general idea of the topic of the article, make a plan. What strategy will help you meet your purpose for reading?

• Use the strategy of reading critically with newspaper articles.

Reading critically means looking at all of the facts presented and deciding how believable they are. Focus on which facts you know you can believe.

During Reading

D Read with a Purpose

Now you're ready for a careful reading of the article.

Directions: Read "Ghastly Deeds of Race Rioters Told." As you read, write down key facts and opinions on the following Critical Reading Chart.

Critical Reading Chart

Key Facts	Key Opinions
40 dead, 500 wounded	Any time the writer puts in his own thoughts,
4,000 troops joined the police.	those are opinions.
Hospitals ran out of room.	". . . The red tongues had blabbed their fill. . . ."
Telephone wires were cut.	"The presence of a black face . . . was a signal
Men, women, and children were killed.	for a carnival of death."
The police fired into the crowd on Wabash.	"But hell was yet to break loose."

NAME

Using the Strategy

Reading critically means understanding the facts presented. As the article is a long one, you'll need to sift through many facts to get to the most important ones.

Directions: Look at your notes and then complete this chart. When you are done, answer the question below.

◄ **Key Facts Chart**

Write three key facts about the riot here:

1. It began in late July, 1919.

2. It started with whites attacking several black boys.

3. It resulted in 40 dead, more than 500 wounded, and countless homes destroyed.

Write three key facts about the African-American rioters here:

1. Their goal was to "avenge" the murder of their brothers and sisters.

2. They attacked "innocent bystanders."

3. They were ruled by mob "hysteria."

Write three key facts about the white rioters here:

1. The presence of a black face in a white neighborhood would touch off a "carnival of death."

2. They traveled in mobs.

3. They attacked "innocent bystanders."

Write your conclusions here: This was a time of terrible violence. Innocent men and women were killed. The victims were both black and white. It seems like most people lost their senses and allowed themselves to be swept up in the mobs.

Are the reporter's sources reliable? The reporter was there, witnessing some of the events, so I'd say he knew what happened. The report has bias, but the description seems pretty trustworthy.

Nonfiction

Understanding How News Stories Are Organized

In a news story, you'll find an overview of the most important facts in the lead.

- **The lead tells you *who, what, where, when, why,* and *how.***

Directions: Reread the *Chicago Defender* lead. Highlight clues about *who, what,* and *where.* Circle clues about *when, why,* and *how.*

> For fully four days this old city has been rocked in a quake of racial antagonism, seared in a blaze of red hate flaming as fiercely as the heat of day—each hour ushering in new stories of slaying, looting, arson, and rape, sending the awful roll of casualties to a grand total of 40 dead and more than 500 wounded, many of them perhaps fatally. A certain madness distinctly indicated in reports of shootings, stabbings, and burning of buildings which literally pour in every minute. Women and children have not been spared. Traffic has been stopped. Phone wires have been cut.

E Connect

Think about how the information in a news story applies to you. This can make the story more interesting and meaningful.

- **To connect to a news story, ask yourself, "How does this apply to me?" or "What else do I know about this subject?"**

Directions: Answer this question about the *Chicago Defender* article.

What else do you know about the Chicago race riots? I know that a lot of the tension came from the fact that the African Americans were much poorer than the whites. The whites, in turn, were very prejudiced against the blacks. I also remember reading that the black soldiers who had recently returned home from World War I were very angry that they had all their rights stripped from them once more. When they were soldiers, they were treated like equals. Once they got home, they were treated like inferiors.

NAME

After Reading

After you finish a news story, reflect on what you've learned.

F Pause and Reflect

At this point, you'll want to return to your original reading purpose.

- **Ask yourself, "Can I answer *who, what, where, when, why,* and *how?*"**

<u>**Directions:**</u> Answer these questions about the *Chicago Defender* story.

Questions

Decide	Yes	No
I can answer <u>who</u>, <u>what</u>, <u>where</u>, <u>when</u>, <u>why</u>, and <u>how</u> questions.	✔	
I know which details are facts and which are opinions.		✔
I understand the article's main idea.	✔	
I can find three details the reporter uses to support the main idea.	✔	

G Reread

If you haven't met your reading purpose, you need to return to the text.

- **A powerful rereading strategy to use with a news story is summarizing.**

<u>**Directions:**</u> Write Summary Notes for the story you read.

Summary Notes

Article headline: "Ghastly Deeds of Race Rioters Told"
Subject: Chicago race riots of 1919
Author's main idea: These riots were brutal and horrible.
Supporting detail #1 Women and children died.
Supporting detail #2 Innocent bystanders were attacked.
Supporting detail #3 As many as 40 people died and 500 were wounded.

Nonfiction

Remember

Remembering the key facts of a news story can help you speak knowledgeably about the subject.

<mark>• **Create a graphic organizer that will help you remember facts and details from the story.**</mark>

Directions: Write the causes of the Chicago race riots in the box on the left. Then, write two or more effects of the riots.

Cause-Effect Organizer

Effect

Causes

Riots between whites and blacks

bigotry
poverty
lack of equality

Effect

40 were killed and more than 500 were injured

NAME _____

Reading a

A biography is the story of a person's life. Most biographers write with two goals in mind: to tell an interesting story and to create an impression of what the person was really like.

Before Reading

The reading process and strategy of looking for cause and effect can help you get more from every biography you read. Practice here with an excerpt from a biography about the circus impresario P. T. Barnum.

 A Set a Purpose

Your primary purpose when reading a biography is to find out as much as you can about the subject and his or her life. Your secondary purpose is to form your own impression of the subject.

• **To set your purpose, ask questions about the biographical subject.**

Directions: Write your purpose for reading a biography about P. T. Barnum. Then, explain what you already know about him.

My purpose: *I want to find out who Barnum was and what he was like.*

_____

Here's what I already know about P. T. Barnum: *He was the "Barnum" in Barnum and Bailey*

Circus.

 B Preview

Preview a biography by examining the front and back covers and table of contents. Look for important information about the subject.

Directions: Preview *The Life of Phineas Taylor Barnum*. Make notes on the stickies as you preview.

Nonfiction

Back Cover

Meet P. T. Barnum—the greatest American entertainer of all time . . .

To many, Phineas Taylor Barnum was the embodiment of the American Dream. Working on the principle that even the most refined audiences loved to be shocked senseless, Barnum presented to a captive world a series of unforgettable exhibits, including:

• Joice Heith, the 161-year-old woman;

• Chang and Eng, the world's "first Siamese twins";

• the Feejee Mermaid, a woman with the body of a fish;

• and "General" Tom Thumb, the world's tiniest soldier.

Throughout his life, Barnum's drive to succeed was powered by his love of money and his craving to be famous. Here is the biography of the man who was himself "The Greatest Show on Earth."

Important facts about the biographical subject:

Barnum loved to shock his audiences.

He was driven by his desire to become rich and famous.

He was himself "The Greatest Show on Earth."

Front Cover

The Life of

Phineas Taylor BARNUM

P. T. Barnum (1810–1891)

by
Joel Benton

The subject of the biography is P. T. Barnum

What is the main time period of the biography? the 1800s

86

NAME

C Plan

After your preview, make a reading plan. Choose a strategy that can help you understand the key events of the subject's life.

- **Use the strategy of looking for cause and effect to help you understand the effect of the subject's life experiences.**

During Reading

D Read with a Purpose

Keep track of key events in the subject's life and how they affected him or her.

Directions: Do a careful reading of the excerpt from the Barnum biography. Make notes on the Cause-Effect Organizer on page 90.

from *The Life of Phineas Taylor Barnum* by Joel Benton

Among the names of great Americans of the nineteenth century, there is scarcely one more familiar to the world than that of the subject of this biography. There are those that stand for higher achievement in literature, science and art, in public life and in the business world. There is none that stands for more notable success in his chosen line, none that recalls more memories of wholesome entertainment, none that is more invested with the fragrance of kindliness and true humanity. His career was, in a large sense, typical of genuine Americanism, of its enterprise and pluck, of its indomitable will and unfailing courage, of its shrewdness, audacity and unerring instinct for success.

Like so many of his famous compatriots, Phineas Taylor Barnum came of good old New England stock. His ancestors were among the builders of the colonies of Massachusetts and Connecticut. His father's father, Ephraim Barnum, was a captain in the War of the Revolution and was distinguished for his valor and for his fervent patriotism. His mother's father, Phineas Taylor, was locally noted as a wag and practical joker. His father, Philo Barnum, was in turn a tailor, a farmer, a storekeeper, and a country tavern keeper and was not particularly prosperous in any of these callings.

Philo Barnum and his wife, Irena Taylor, lived at Bethel, Connecticut, and there, on July 5, 1810, their first child was born. He was named Phineas Taylor Barnum, after his maternal grandfather; and the latter, in return for the compliment, bestowed upon his first grandchild at his christening the title-deeds of a "landed estate," five acres in extent, known as Ivy Island, and situated in that part of Bethel known as the "Plum Trees."

Nonfiction

from *The Life of Phineas Taylor Barnum* by Joel Benton

In his early years the boy led the life of the average New England farmer's son of that period. He drove the cows to and from the pasture, shelled corn, weeded the garden, and "did up chores." As he grew older he rode the horse in plowing corn, raked hay, wielded the shovel and the hoe, and chopped wood. At six years old he began to go to school—the typical district school. "The first date," he once said, "I remember inscribing upon my writing-book was 1818." The ferule, or the birch-rod, was in those days the assistant schoolmaster, and young Barnum made its acquaintance. He was, however, an apt and ready scholar, particularly excelling in mathematics. One night, when he was ten years old, he was called out of bed by his teacher, who had made a wager with a neighbor that Barnum could calculate the number of feet in a load of wood in five minutes. Barnum did it in less than two minutes, to the delight of his teacher and the astonishment of the neighbor.

At an early age he manifested a strong development of the good old Yankee organ of acquisitiveness. Before he was five years old he had begun to hoard pennies and "fourpences," and at six years old he was able to exchange his copper bits for a whole silver dollar, the possession of which made him feel richer than he ever felt afterward in all his life. Nor did he lay the dollar away in a napkin, but used it in business to gain more. He would get ten cents a day for riding a horse before the plow, and he would add it to his capital. On holidays other boys spent all their savings, but not so he. Such days were to him opportunities for gain, not for squandering. At the fair or training of troops, or other festivity, he would peddle candy and cakes, home-made, or sometimes cherry rum, and by the end of the day would be a dollar or two richer than at its beginning. "By the time I was twelve years old," he tells us, "I was the owner of a sheep and a calf, and should soon, no doubt, have become a small Croesus had not my father kindly permitted me to purchase my own clothing, which somewhat reduced my little store."

At ten years of age, realizing himself to be a "landed proprietor" through the christening gift of his waggish grandsire, young Barnum set out to survey his estate, which he had not yet seen. He had heard much of "Ivy Island." His grandfather had often, in the presence of the neighbors, spoken of him as the richest child in the town, since he owned the whole of Ivy Island, the richest farm in the State. His parents hoped he would use his wealth wisely, and "do something for the family" when he entered upon the possession of it; and the neighbors were fearful lest he should grow too proud to associate with their children.

The boy took all this in good faith, and his eager curiosity to behold his estate was greatly increased, and he asked his father to let him go thither. "At last," says Barnum, "he promised I should do so in a few days, as we should be getting some hay near 'Ivy Island.' The wished-for day arrived, and my father told me that as we were to mow an adjoining meadow, I might visit my property in company with the hired man during the 'nooning.' My grandfather reminded me that it was to his bounty I was indebted

from *The Life of Phineas Taylor Barnum* by Joel Benton

for this wealth, and that had not my name been Phineas I might never have been proprietor of 'Ivy Island.' To this my mother added:

"'Now, Taylor, don't become so excited when you see your property as to let your joy make you sick, for remember, rich as you are, that it will be eleven years before you can come into possession of your fortune.'

"She added much more good advice, to all of which I promised to be calm and reasonable, and not to allow my pride to prevent me from speaking to my brothers and sisters when I returned home.

"When we arrived at the meadow, which was in that part of the 'Plum Trees' known as 'East Swamp,' I asked my father where 'Ivy Island' was.

"'Yonder, at the north end of this meadow, where you see those beautiful trees rising in the distance.'

"All the forenoon I turned grass as fast as two men could cut it, and after a hasty repast at noon, one of our hired men, a good-natured Irishman, named Edmund, took an axe on his shoulder and announced that he was ready to accompany me to 'Ivy Island.' We started, and as we approached the north end of the meadow we found the ground swampy and wet and were soon obliged to leap from bog to bog on our route. A mis-step brought me up to my middle in water, and to add to the dilemma a swarm of hornets attacked me. Attaining the altitude of another bog I was cheered by the assurance that there was only a quarter of a mile of this kind of travel to the edge of my property. I waded on. In about fifteen minutes more, after floundering through the morass, I found myself half-drowned, hornet-stung, mud covered, and out of breath, on comparatively dry land.

"'Never mind, my boy,' said Edmund, 'we have only to cross this little creek, and ye'll be upon your own valuable property.'

"We were on the margin of a stream, the banks of which were thickly covered with alders. I now discovered the use of Edmund's axe, for he felled a small oak to form a temporary bridge to my 'Island' property. Crossing over, I proceeded to the center of my domain. I saw nothing but a few stunted ivies and straggling trees. The truth flashed upon me. I had been the laughing-stock of the family and neighborhood for years. My valuable 'Ivy Island' was an almost inaccessible, worthless bit of barren land, and while I stood deploring my sudden downfall, a huge black snake (one of my tenants) approached me with upraised head. I gave one shriek and rushed for the bridge.

"This was my first and last visit to 'Ivy Island.' My father asked me 'how I liked my property?,' and I responded that I would sell it pretty cheap."

NAME ....

FOR USE WITH PAGES 193–209

Cause-Effect Organizer

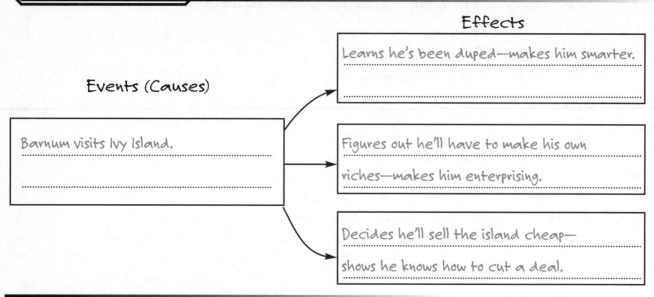

Effects

Learns he's been duped—makes him smarter.

Events (Causes)

Barnum visits Ivy Island.

Figures out he'll have to make his own riches—makes him enterprising.

Decides he'll sell the island cheap— shows he knows how to cut a deal.

Look for Information

Often you will need to make inferences about how an event affected the subject's life. Use an Inference Chart to organize your thoughts.

Directions: Read the excerpts about Barnum in the chart below. Then note what you can infer about him.

Inference Chart

Text Details	What I've Inferred about Barnum
One night, when he was ten years old, he was called out of bed by his teacher, who had made a wager with a neighbor that Barnum could calculate the number of feet in a load of wood in five minutes. Barnum did it in less than two minutes.	He was very smart and had a good head for figures. I'm sure this helped him later, when he became a showman.
Before he was five years old he had begun to hoard pennies and "fourpences," and at six years old he was able to exchange his copper bits for a whole silver dollar, the possession of which made him feel richer than he ever felt afterward in all his life.	The book jacket says that he was driven by a desire to become rich. I see he started earning and saving money when he was very young.
"This was my first and last visit to 'Ivy Island.' My father asked me 'how I liked my property?,' and I responded that I would sell it pretty cheap."	I think this story shows that Barnum was sort of impulsive but had a good sense of humor. Right away he decides to sell the island, but he admits that it will be for "pretty cheap." This is a funny line coming out of an eleven-year-old.

Understanding How Biographies Are Organized

Good biographers include stories that can help the reader form a strong impression of the subject.

• **Think of a biography as a series of stories that offer clues about the subject's personality.**

Directions: What is your impression thus far of P. T. Barnum? Make notes on the following Character Map.

> **Character Map**

How he acts and feels

He has a lot of self-confidence. He knows what he wants and goes after it. Instead of relying on others to do the work, he jumps in there and does it himself.

How others feel about him

They seem to like him, but they don't mind playing the Ivy Island trick on him. The adults respect his academic abilities.

P. T. Barnum

How he looks and talks

He's a fast talker. This part of the biography only deals with his early childhood, but you can tell that he's going to end up being a wheeler-dealer.

How I feel about him

I can tell that he's really enterprising. He's the type who can make a profit on just about anything.

E Connect

The personal connections you make when reading a biography can sharpen your impression of the subject.

• **Connect to a biography by asking yourself, "How do I feel about the subject?"**

Directions: Reread this passage from the biography. Then, make your observations on the sticky.

At an early age he manifested a strong development of the good old Yankee organ of acquisitiveness. Before he was five years old he had begun to hoard pennies and "fourpences," and at six years old he was able to exchange his copper bits for a whole silver dollar, the possession of which made him feel richer than he ever felt afterward in all his life. Nor did he lay the dollar away in a napkin, but used it in business to gain more. He would get ten cents a day for riding a horse before the plow, and he would add it to his capital. On holidays other boys spent all their savings, but not so he. Such days were to him opportunities for gain, not for squandering.

P. T. Barnum reminds me of my little brother. He's a saver, not a spender, too. When I need money, I go to him for a loan.

After Reading

When you finish a biography, think about what you've learned.

 ## Pause and Reflect

Ask yourself questions about the biographical subject and your purpose for reading.

- **To reflect on your purpose, ask yourself, "Can I speak knowledgeably about the biographical subject?"**

Directions: Answer these questions about P. T. Barnum.

Questions

Can I name several events in the subject's life? Yes.

Do I understand how these events affected the subject? Yes.

Do I have a sense of what the person was really like? Yes.

Can I say how I feel about the subject? Yes.

Can I support how I feel with evidence from the text? Maybe.

 ## Reread

No reader can absorb every detail on a single reading. If you find you don't have a clear impression of the subject, you'll need to do some rereading.

- **The rereading strategy of outlining can help you find and process additional details about the biographical subject.**

Directions: Reread key parts of the excerpt. Then, write details about P. T. Barnum on this Outline.

Outline

P. T. Barnum: Early Years
I. Important event #1: Grandfather bestows "Ivy Island."
A. Christening gift for his namesake
B. Allows P. T. to think it is a great estate
II. Important event #2: P. T. begins school.
A. Shows aptitude with numbers
B. Beaten by schoolmaster for misbehavior
III. Important event #3: P. T. visits Ivy Island.
A. Learns that it is unusable swampland
B. Understands people have been toying with him

H Remember

Good readers remember what they've read. Making a map or a sketch can help.

• **Creating a map or sketch can help you retain what you've learned about the subject.**

Directions: Make a sketch of P. T. Barnum on Ivy Island.

Sketch

Reading a Memoir

In a memoir, a writer describes some important events from his or her life. The writer reflects on the meaning of those events and their influence.

Before Reading

Here, you'll use the reading process and the strategy of synthesizing to help you read an excerpt from Harriet Jacobs's memoir, *Incidents in the Life of a Slave Girl*.

 A ### Set a Purpose

Your purpose in reading a memoir is twofold. First, you need to understand the life experiences the writer describes. Second, you need to form your own impression of the writer and the people, places, times, and events described.

> • **To set your purpose, ask two questions about the writer of the memoir.**

Directions: Ask two questions about Harriet Jacobs or her memoir.

Purpose question #1 *What kind of life did Harriet Jacobs have?*

Purpose question #2 *How do I feel about her and about the people, places, times, and events*

she describes?

 B ### Preview

After you set your purpose, begin your preview of the memoir. Look carefully at the front and back covers of the book. What information can you find that helps you meet your purpose?

Directions: Preview the front and back covers of *Incidents in the Life of a Slave Girl* on the next page. Make notes on the stickies.

NAME

Back Cover

Reader, be assured this narrative is no fiction. I am aware that some of my adventures may seem incredible; but they are, nevertheless, strictly true. I have not exaggerated the wrongs inflicted by slavery; on the contrary, my descriptions fall far short of the facts. . . .

I wish I were more competent to the task I have undertaken. But I trust my readers will excuse deficiencies in consideration of circumstances. I was born and reared in slavery; and I remained in a slave state twenty-seven years. Since I have been in the North, it has been necessary for me to work diligently for my own support, and the education of my children. This has not left me much leisure to make up for the loss of early opportunities to improve myself; and it has compelled me to write these pages at irregular intervals, whenever I could snatch an hour from household duties.

Front Cover

INCIDENTS
IN THE
LIFE OF A SLAVE GIRL.
WRITTEN BY HERSELF.

"Northerners know nothing at all about slavery. They think it is perpetual bondage only. They have no conception of the depth of degradation involved in that word, SLAVERY; if they had, they would never cease their efforts until so horrible a system was overthrown."
A WOMAN OF NORTH CAROLINA

Important details I noticed:

detail #1 Everything Jacobs says in the book is true.

detail #2 She apologizes for the roughness of her writing.

detail #3 She was a slave for 27 years.

The title Incidents in the Life of a Slave Girl

The quotes tell me Jacobs believes slavery is a degradation, which is probably why she has included the quote from the North Carolina woman.

C Plan

When you've finished previewing, make a reading plan that will help you meet your purpose.

• **Use the strategy of synthesizing to help you get a feel for the "big picture" the writer is presenting.**

Synthesizing is a little like putting together a jigsaw puzzle. When all the pieces are in place, you have a completed picture. In a memoir, the puzzle pieces are the events the writer describes. The big picture is the self-portrait the writer is creating from all the events narrated.

During Reading

D Read with a Purpose

As you read, note the key experiences in the writer's life. Think about how the experiences affected the writer.

Directions: Do a careful reading of the excerpt from Harriet Jacobs's memoir. Make notes on the Key Word or Topic Notes on page 99.

from *Incidents in the Life of a Slave Girl* by Harriet Jacobs

I was born a slave; but I never knew it till six years of happy childhood had passed away. My father was a carpenter, and considered so intelligent and skillful in his trade, that, when buildings out of the common line were to be erected, he was sent for from long distances, to be head workman.

On condition of paying his mistress two hundred dollars a year, and supporting himself, he was allowed to work at his trade, and manage his own affairs. His strongest wish was to purchase his children; but, though he several times offered his hard earnings for that purpose, he never succeeded.

In complexion my parents were a light shade of brownish yellow, and were termed mulattoes. They lived together in a comfortable home; and, though we were all slaves, I was so fondly shielded that I never dreamed I was a piece of merchandise, trusted to them for safe keeping, and liable to be demanded of them at any moment.

I had one brother, William, who was two years younger than myself—a bright, affectionate child. I had also a great treasure in my maternal grandmother, who was a remarkable woman in many respects. She was the daughter of a planter in South Carolina, who, at his death, left her mother and his three children free, with money to go to St. Augustine, where they had relatives. It was during the Revolutionary War; and they were captured on their passage, carried back, and sold to different purchasers.

Such was the story my grandmother used to tell me; but I do not remember all the particulars. She was a little girl when she was captured and sold to the keeper of a

© GREAT SOURCE. ALL RIGHTS RESERVED.

◇ from *Incidents in the Life of a Slave Girl* by Harriet Jacobs ◇

large hotel. I have often heard her tell how hard she fared during childhood. But as she grew older she evinced so much intelligence, and was so faithful, that her master and mistress could not help seeing it was for their interest to take care of such a valuable piece of property.

Stop and Organize

Make some notes about Jacobs on your Key Word or Topic Notes on page 99.

She became an indispensable personage in the household, officiating in all capacities, from cook and wet nurse to seamstress. She was much praised for her cooking; and her nice crackers became so famous in the neighborhood that many people were desirous of obtaining them. In consequence of numerous requests of this kind, she asked permission of her mistress to bake crackers at night, after all the household work was done; and she obtained leave to do it, provided she would clothe herself and her children from the profits.

Upon these terms, after working hard all day for her mistress, she began her midnight bakings, assisted by her two oldest children. The business proved profitable; and each year she laid by a little, which was saved for a fund to purchase her children. Her master died, and the property was divided among his heirs. The widow had her dower in the hotel, which she continued to keep open. My grandmother remained in her service as a slave; but her children were divided among her master's children. As she had five, Benjamin, the youngest one, was sold, in order that each heir might have an equal portion of dollars and cents.

There was so little difference in our ages that he seemed more like my brother than my uncle. He was a bright, handsome lad, nearly white; for he inherited the complexion my grandmother had derived from Anglo-Saxon ancestors. Though only ten years old, seven hundred and twenty dollars were paid for him. His sale was a terrible blow to my grandmother; but she was naturally hopeful, and she went to work with renewed energy, trusting in time to be able to purchase some of her children.

She had laid up three hundred dollars, which her mistress one day begged as a loan, promising to pay her soon. The reader probably knows that no promise or writing given to a slave is legally binding; for, according to Southern laws, a slave, being property, can hold no property. When my grandmother lent her hard earnings to her mistress, she trusted solely to her honor. The honor of a slaveholder to a slave!

Stop and Organize

Make more notes about Jacobs on the Key Word or Topic Notes on page 99.

from *Incidents in the Life of a Slave Girl* by Harriet Jacobs

To this good grandmother I was indebted for many comforts. My brother Willie and I often received portions of the crackers, cakes, and preserves, she made to sell; and after we ceased to be children we were indebted to her for many more important services.

Such were the unusually fortunate circumstances of my early childhood. When I was six years old, my mother died; and then, for the first time, I learned, by the talk around me, that I was a slave.

My mother's mistress was the daughter of my grandmother's mistress. She was the foster sister of my mother; they were both nourished at my grandmother's breast. In fact, my mother had been weaned at three months old, that the babe of the mistress might obtain sufficient food. They played together as children; and, when they became women, my mother was a most faithful servant to her whiter foster sister. On her death-bed her mistress promised that her children should never suffer for any thing; and during her lifetime she kept her word.

They all spoke kindly of my dead mother, who had been a slave merely in name, but in nature was noble and womanly. I grieved for her, and my young mind was troubled with the thought of who would now take care of me and my little brother. I was told that my home was now to be with her mistress; and I found it a happy one. No toilsome or disagreeable duties were imposed upon me. My mistress was so kind to me that I was always glad to do her bidding, and proud to labor for her as much as my young years would permit.

I would sit by her side for hours, sewing diligently, with a heart as free from care as that of any free-born white child. When she thought I was tired, she would send me out to run and jump; and away I bounded, to gather berries or flowers to decorate her room. Those were happy days—too happy to last. The slave child had no thought for the morrow; but there came that blight, which too surely waits on every human being born to be a chattel.

When I was nearly twelve years old, my kind mistress sickened and died. As I saw the cheek grow paler, and the eye more glassy, how earnestly I prayed in my heart that she might live! I loved her; for she had been almost like a mother to me. My prayers were not answered. She died, and they buried her in the little churchyard, where, day after day, my tears fell upon her grave.

Stop and Organize

Make more notes about Jacobs on your Key Word or Topic Notes on page 99.

I was sent to spend a week with my grandmother. I was now old enough to begin to think of the future; and again and again I asked myself what they would do with me. I felt sure I should never find another mistress so kind as the one who was gone. She had promised my dying mother that her children should never suffer for any

◣ from *Incidents in the Life of a Slave Girl* by Harriet Jacobs ◢

thing; and when I remembered that, and recalled her many proofs of attachment to me, I could not help having some hopes that she had left me free. My friends were almost certain it would be so. They thought she would be sure to do it, on account of my mother's love and faithful service. But, alas! we all know that the memory of a faithful slave does not avail much to save her children from the auction block.

After a brief period of suspense, the will of my mistress was read, and we learned that she had bequeathed me to her sister's daughter, a child of five years old. So vanished our hopes. My mistress had taught me the precepts of God's Word: "Thou shalt love thy neighbor as thyself." "Whatsoever ye would that men should do unto you, do ye even so unto them." But I was her slave, and I suppose she did not recognize me as her neighbor.

I would give much to blot out from my memory that one great wrong. As a child, I loved my mistress; and, looking back on the happy days I spent with her, I try to think with less bitterness of this act of injustice. While I was with her, she taught me to read and spell; and for this privilege, which so rarely falls to the lot of a slave, I bless her memory.

She possessed but few slaves; and at her death those were all distributed among her relatives. Five of them were my grandmother's children, and had shared the same milk that nourished her mother's children. Notwithstanding my grandmother's long and faithful service to her owners, not one of her children escaped the auction block. These God-breathing machines are no more, in the sight of their masters, than the cotton they plant, or the horses they tend.

◣ **Key Word or Topic Notes**

Key Topics	Notes from Reading
period the writer focuses on	her years as a slave
physical surroundings	North Carolina plantation; southern hotel
work	servant to the mistress of the house
major problems	She is not free. She knows that she or members of her family
	may be sold at any time. Her beloved mistress dies, and she
	learns that she will be auctioned.
personality and character	She is intelligent and strong of heart. She clearly understands
	the people and events of her life. She also seems angry. In the
	final paragraph, she shows she is bitter and not afraid to say so.

Using the Strategy

Use the strategy of synthesizing to help you "see" the portrait the writer has created.

Directions: Complete this Web about Harriet Jacobs. Refer to your notes as needed.

Web

Proof: Knows what she wants from life

Proof: Understands the horror of her situation

Proof: Can offer detailed descriptions of her surroundings and actions

Trait: Intelligent

Trait: Highly observant

HARRIET JACOBS

Proof: Sees and makes note of grief, anger, heartache, worry, and despair in herself and in others

Trait: Loyal to family

Proof: Speaks warmly about all that her grandmother did for her and for her mother before her

Proof: Repeatedly describes the exceptional nature of her family members

NAME ....

Understanding How Memoirs Are Organized

Most writers use chronological order to structure their memoirs. This means that they describe the events in the order in which they occurred. Then, they explain their thoughts and feelings about the events.

• **Sequence Notes can help you track the major events in the writer's life.**

Directions: Record four key events from Jacobs's life on this organizer.

◀ **Sequence Notes**

| She is born a slave, but she doesn't realize it. | At age six, her mother dies, and she realizes she's a slave. | Harriet begins working as a servant for the mistress. | The mistress dies, and Harriet knows she will be sold. |

Nonfiction

E **Connect**

At this point, think about the second part of your reading purpose: to form an impression of the writer and the people, places, and events she describes.

• **Connect to a memoir by recording your thoughts and feelings about the writer.**

Directions: On the lines below, write your impressions of Harriet Jacobs. Support what you say with "proof" from the excerpt.

I have to say that I really admire her. She is very frank in her descriptions and has some keen

insights about slavery to offer. I really like what she says at the end of the chapter. Even though

she loved her mistress, she recognizes that to her and other women, slaves were no more "than the

cotton they plant, or the horses they tend."

....

....

....

....

After Reading

Take the time now to think about what you've learned.

F Pause and Reflect

At this point, you'll want to return to your reading purpose and think about whether you've accomplished what you set out to do.

> • **After you finish a memoir, ask yourself, "How well did I meet my purpose?"**

Directions: Answer these questions about Harriet Jacobs.

Looking Back

Have I been able to form an impression of the writer? *Yes, I think I have a good understanding of what she was like, at least as a child. I'd like to find out more about her.*

Do I have a clear understanding of the people, places, times, and events the writer describes? *Yes. Harriet Jacobs gives a really clear, detailed description of the people and events of her early life.*

Do I know how I feel about the writer? *Yes. I knew right away that Jacobs was a person I would admire. There is plenty of evidence in the chapter that she is a person worth admiring.*

Do I understand the purpose of the memoir? *I'm not sure. I need to think some more about why Jacobs wrote her memoir. I need to look for clues about her purpose.*

G Reread

If you feel you haven't met your purpose, spend a few minutes rereading. Choose a rereading strategy that will help you locate the information you need.

> • **A powerful rereading strategy to use with a memoir is visualizing and thinking aloud.**

When you visualize, you make mental pictures of what you are reading. When you think aloud, you talk to yourself about what you've learned.

Directions: Make a quick sketch of the "midnight baking" Jacobs describes. Show both Harriet and her grandmother in the sketch. Then, write a Think Aloud that explains what they're doing and why they're doing it.

> **Visualizing**

This sketch shows Harriet's grandmother baking crackers at midnight. Harriet's grandmother cooked at this hour in order to earn extra money. She planned to use the money to purchase her children's freedom. When she had $300.00 saved, however, her mistress begged her for a loan and then never repaid the money.

H **Remember**

If you've read a memoir for a class assignment, you need to find a way to remember the most important details and your impression of the writer.

• **Writing a book review can help you retain what you've learned.**

Directions: Write a review of this chapter from *Incidents in the Life of a Slave Girl*. Open with your impression of Harriet Jacobs. Then, explain why you would or would not like to read more of her story.

> **Book Review**

Incidents in the Life of a Slave Girl

After reading Chapter I of <u>Incidents in the Life of a Slave Girl</u>, I have a clear impression of what Harriet Jacobs was like. She was intelligent, observant, and keenly aware of the injustice of slavery. In this chapter, Jacobs narrates the early years of her life and how she finally became aware that she was a slave. Even as a young girl, she understood the horror of the auction block and knew that she would do everything she could to avoid it. Clearly this is a book that is well worth reading.

Nonfiction

Focus on Persuasive Writing

Persuasive writing makes an argument or attempts to prove something is true. Your job is to understand and evaluate the argument the writer presents. A three-step plan will help.

Step 1 Find the topic.

As a first step, find the topic. Ask yourself, "What is the writer mostly talking about?"

Directions: Read this editorial. Make notes on the stickies.

Cell Phone and Beeper Ban for the Birds

Yesterday morning, Principal Jameel Roberts announced a school-wide ban on pagers and cell phones. The ban will go into effect Monday of next week. Beginning that day, teachers are required to confiscate any cell phone or pager they see and turn it over to the principal's office. Repeat offenders will be suspended.

Principal Roberts says that this "digital ban" is in the students' best interest. He told an assembly of 10th, 11th, and 12th grade students that he is instituting the ban because cell phones and pagers are disruptive and distracting. He also expressed concern that in some schools, students use these digital devices to conduct illegal activities.

But is it fair for Principal Roberts to punish students at our school for the misdeeds of students at other schools? Here at Emerson High, there is no evidence that students are using cell phones and pagers for illegal activities. In fact, most students use their cell phones and pagers for *admirable* activities like setting up study groups, consulting with each other about missed assignments, and so on.

Furthermore, there is no evidence that cell phones or pagers are disruptive. As a courtesy, most students turn their electronics off or activate a "silent ring" feature when they are in class. They don't sit and talk on the phone in the middle of the class or send pages to friends while the teacher is lecturing. It just doesn't happen.

As a final point, I wonder how the digital ban will affect the staff of

NAME

"Cell Phone and Beeper Ban for the Birds"

Emerson High. How many teachers carry cell phones or pagers with them in their pockets or purses? It's a safe bet that most of them do. Teachers need these devices for the same reason students do: to keep in touch.

So it would seem that Principal Roberts needs to reconsider his digital ban. Students need cell phones, teachers need cell phones, and even school principals need cell phones. What's the point of fighting it?

The title/headline is: Cell Phone and Beeper Ban for the Birds

The topic is a school-wide ban on cell phones and pagers.

Step 2 Find the assertion and support.

The assertion is a statement of belief that the writer explains and supports.

Directions: Reread the editorial. Write the author's assertion on the lines below.

The writer's assertion is that a ban on cell phones and pagers is unfair and unnecessary.

Step 3 Evaluate the argument.

As a final step, decide how you feel about the argument.

Directions: Complete this Argument Chart. Write the viewpoint and evidence. Then evaluate the argument.

Argument Chart

Assertion	Support	My Opinion
Principal Roberts should rethink his ban on cell phones and beepers.	Students use cell phones for admirable, not illegal, activities. Students are conscious about keeping their cell phone or pager quiet. Teachers need cell phones and pagers, too.	The writer's assertion is clear. I would have liked to see more support, maybe in the form of statistics. For example, how many cell phone- or beeper-related problems does the school have in a year?

Nonfiction

Focus on Speeches

When you read a speech, try to imagine how the speaker sounds. Then, use the reading process to understand and evaluate the speaker's message.

Step 1 Learn about the speaker and purpose of the speech.

Your first step will be to find out what you can about the speaker and the purpose of the speech.

Directions: Read this speech. Make notes on the Web that follows.

"Let Me Be a Free Man" by Chief Joseph, Nez Percé Nation

Chief Joseph (1840–1904) of the Nez Percé Nation is remembered for his dramatic effort to move members of his tribe to Canada after the news that whites would be permitted to settle the Oregon Territory. In 1877, Chief Joseph and his followers were captured and forced onto a barren reservation in Oklahoma. In the speech that follows, he begs for the right for his people to remain free.

If the white man wants to live in peace with the Indian, he can live in peace. . . . Treat all men alike. Give them all the same law. Give them all an even chance to live and grow. All men were made by the same Great Spirit Chief. They are all brothers. The Earth is the mother of all people, and all people should have equal rights upon it. . . .Let me be a free man, free to travel, free to stop, free to work, free to trade . . . where I choose my own teachers, free to follow the religion of my fathers, free to think and talk and act for myself, and I will obey every law, or submit to the penalty.

NAME ....

Web

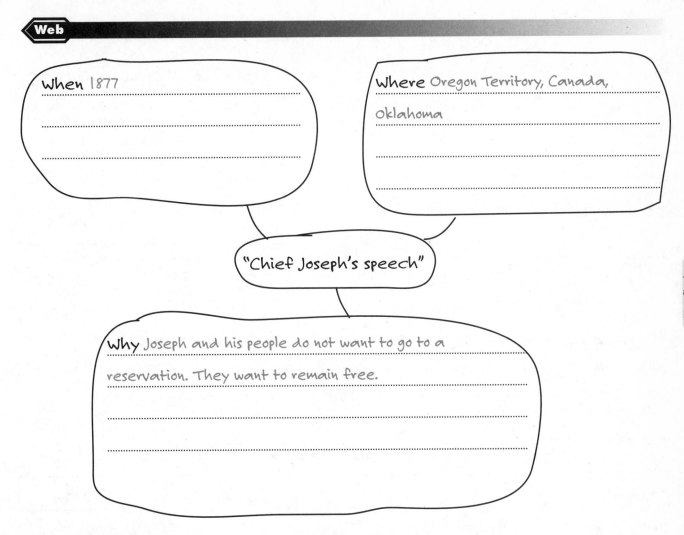

When 1877

Where Oregon Territory, Canada, Oklahoma

"Chief Joseph's speech"

Why Joseph and his people do not want to go to a reservation. They want to remain free.

Step 2 Understand the organization.

Not every line in a speech is equally important. Look for key lines and mark them. They can help you figure out the speaker's message.

Directions: Reread Chief Joseph's speech. Highlight the most important lines.

Step 3 Find the viewpoint.

The speaker's opinion or main idea is called the "viewpoint." Use this formula to find the viewpoint:

Subject of the Speech + Speaker's Opinion of the Subject = The Speaker's Main Idea or Viewpoint

Directions: Use the formula to find the viewpoint of Chief Joseph's speech.

Subject of the Speech + Speaker's Opinion of the Subject = The Speaker's Main Idea or Viewpoint

moving to a   He wants to remain free.   Chief Joseph and his people should

reservation   be permitted to remain free.

Step 4 Locate support for the viewpoint.

A good speaker will support his or her viewpoint with plenty of details.

Directions: Make notes about Chief Joseph's viewpoint and support on this Evidence Organizer.

Evidence Organizer

Viewpoint: Chief Joseph and his people should be permitted to remain free.

Detail 1	Detail 2	Detail 3	Detail 4
Whites and Indians can live together in peace.	All men should have the same law.	All men were made by the same Great Spirit.	If he is permitted to remain free, Chief Joseph will obey every law and pay every penalty.

NAME ....

Reading a Short Story

Reading a short story can be one of life's greatest pleasures. But there is no pleasure without comprehension. The reading process can help you understand what you're reading.

Before Reading

Let the reading process and the strategy of synthesizing help you read and respond to the short story "The Last Leaf" by O. Henry.

A Set a Purpose

Beginning by setting your purpose will help you get more from the short story you're about to read.

• **To set your purpose, ask important questions about the major elements of the story.**

<u>Directions:</u> Write your purpose questions in the second column.

Purpose Chart

Element	My Questions
characters	Who are the major characters?
setting	Where and when does the story take place?
plot	What happens in the story?
dialogue	What do the characters talk about?
point of view	From whose point of view is the story told?

Fiction

B Preview

You read better if you know what to expect. A preview can clue you in as to what's to come.

Directions: Preview "The Last Leaf." Answer the questions that follow. Then, make a prediction about the story.

Preview Chart

Who is the author of the story? O. Henry

What did you find out about the point of view? There is a narrator who observes the action and tells the thoughts of one of the characters—Sue.

What did you learn from the first few paragraphs? The story takes place in Washington Square in Greenwich Village, which I think is in New York City. There are at least two characters: Sue and Johnsy.

What repeated words did you notice? artist, art, studio

My prediction: I think either Sue or Johnsy is going to get sick and possibly die. My clue is that the background section calls this a "sentimental" story.

"The Last Leaf" by O. Henry

What you need to know . . .

THE SELECTION In "The Last Leaf," a young woman struggles to help her friend recover from a deadly case of pneumonia.

THE AUTHOR O. Henry was the pen name for William Sidney Porter (1862–1910). He was one of the best short story writers in American history. His love for ordinary men and women who live ordinary lives resonates in the great majority of his stories. "The Last Leaf" is one of his most sentimental—and popular—stories.

THE THEME determination

LITERARY FOCUS characterization

FURTHER READING "The Gift of the Magi" and "The Ransom of Red Chief"

In a little district west of Washington Square the streets have run crazy and broken themselves into small strips called "places." These "places" make strange angles and curves. One street crosses itself a time or two. An artist once discovered a valuable possibility in this street. Suppose a collector with a bill for paints, paper, and canvas should, in traversing this route, suddenly meet himself coming back, without a cent having been paid on account!

So, to quaint old Greenwich Village the art people soon came prowling, hunting for north windows and eighteenth-century gables and Dutch attics and low rents. Then they imported some pewter mugs and a chafing dish or two from Sixth Avenue, and became a "colony."

At the top of a squatty, three-story brick house Sue and Johnsy had their studio. "Johnsy" was familiar for Joanna. One was from Maine; the other from California. They had met at the *table d'hôte* of an Eighth street "Delmonico's" and found their tastes in art and chicory salad so congenial that the joint studio resulted.

That was in May. In November a cold, unseen stranger, whom the doctors called Pneumonia, stalked about the colony, touching one here and there with his icy finger. Over on the east side this ravager strode boldly, smiting his victims by scores, but his feet trod slowly through the maze of the narrow and moss-grown "places."

Stop and Organize
Make some notes in the "Setting" section of the Synthesizing Chart on page 116.

Mr. Pneumonia was not what you would call a chivalric old gentleman. A mite of a little woman with blood thinned by California zephyrs was hardly fair game for the red-fisted, short-breathed old duffer. But Johnsy he smote; and she lay, scarcely moving, on her painted iron bedstead, looking through the small Dutch windowpanes at the blank side of the next brick house.

One morning the busy doctor invited Sue into the hallway with a shaggy, grey eyebrow.

"She has one chance in, let us say, ten," he said, as he shook down the mercury in his clinical thermometer. "And that chance is for her to want to live. This way people have of lining-up on the side of the undertaker makes the entire pharmacopoeia[1] look silly. Your little lady has made up her mind that she's not going to get well. Has she anything on her mind?"

"She wanted to paint the Bay of Naples some day," said Sue.

"Paint? Bosh! Has she anything on her mind worth thinking about twice—a man, for instance?"

"A man?" said Sue, with a twang in her voice. "Is a man worth—but no, doctor; there is nothing of the kind."

"Well, it is the weakness, then," said the doctor. "I will do all that science, so far as it may filter through my efforts, can accomplish. But whenever my patient begins to count the carriages in her funeral procession I subtract 50 percent from the curative power of medicines. If you will get her to ask one question about the new winter styles in cloak sleeves I will promise you a one-in-five chance for her, instead of one in ten."

1. **pharmacopoeia**—the book of drugs and pharmaceuticals a doctor might prescribe.

"The Last Leaf" by O. Henry

After the doctor had gone, Sue went into the workroom and cried a Japanese napkin to a pulp. Then she swaggered into Johnsy's room with her drawing-board, whistling ragtime.

Johnsy lay, scarcely making a ripple under the bedclothes, with her face toward the window. Sue stopped whistling, thinking she was asleep.

She arranged her board and began a pen-and-ink drawing to illustrate a magazine story. Young artists must pave their way to Art by drawing pictures for magazine stories that young authors write to pave their way to Literature.

As Sue was sketching a pair of elegant horse show riding trousers and a monocle on the figure of the hero, an Idaho cowboy, she heard a low sound, several times repeated. She went quickly to the bedside.

Johnsy's eyes were open wide. She was looking out the window and counting backward.

"Twelve," she said, and a little later "eleven"; and then "ten," and "nine"; and then "eight" and "seven," almost together.

Sue looked solicitously out the window. What was there to count? There was only a bare, dreary yard to be seen, and the blank side of the brick house twenty feet away. An old, old ivy vine, gnarled and decayed at the roots, climbed half-way up the brick wall. The cold breath of autumn had stricken its leaves from the vine until its skeleton branches clung, almost bare, to the crumbling bricks.

"What is it, dear?" asked Sue.

"Six," said Johnsy, in almost a whisper. "They're falling faster now. Three days ago there were almost a hundred. It made my head ache to count them. But now it's easy. There goes another one. There are only five left now."

"Five what, dear? Tell your Sudie."

"Leaves. On the ivy vine. When the last one falls I must go too. I've known that for three days. Didn't the doctor tell you?"

"Oh, I never heard of such nonsense!" complained Sue, with magnificent scorn. "What have old ivy leaves to do with your getting well? And you used to love that vine so, you naughty girl. Don't be a goosey. Why, the doctor told me this morning that your chances for getting well real soon were let's see exactly what he said—he said the chances were ten to one! Why, that's almost as good a chance as we have in New York when we ride on the street cars or walk past a new building. Try to take some broth now, and let Sudie go back to her drawing, so she can sell the editor man with it, and buy port wine for her sick child, and pork chops for her greedy self."

"You needn't get any more wine," said Johnsy, keeping her eyes fixed out the window. "There goes another. No, I don't want any broth. That leaves just four. I want to see the last one fall before it gets dark. Then I'll go too."

"Johnsy, dear," said Sue, bending over her, "will you promise me to keep your eyes closed, and not look out the window until I am done working? I must hand these drawings in by to-morrow. I need the light, or I would draw the shade down."

Fiction

"The Last Leaf" by O. Henry

"Couldn't you draw in the other room?" asked Johnsy coldly.

"I'd rather be here by you," said Sue. "Besides, I don't want you to keep looking at those silly ivy leaves."

"Tell me as soon as you have finished," said Johnsy, closing her eyes, and lying white and still as a fallen statue, "because I want to see the last one fall. I'm tired of waiting. I'm tired of thinking. I want to turn loose my hold on everything, and go sailing down, down, just like one of those poor, tired leaves."

"Try to sleep," said Sue. "I must call Behrman up to be my model for the old hermit miner. I'll not be gone a minute. Don't try to move till I come back."

Old Behrman was a painter who lived on the ground floor beneath them. He was past sixty and had a Michelangelo's Moses beard curling down from the head of a satyr along the body of an imp. Behrman was a failure in art. Forty years he had wielded the brush without getting near enough to touch the hem of his Mistress's robe. He had been always about to paint a masterpiece, but had never yet begun it. For several years he had painted nothing except now and then a daub in the line of commerce or advertising. He earned a little by serving as a model to those young artists in the colony who could not pay the price of a professional. He drank gin to excess, and still talked of his coming masterpiece. For the rest he was a fierce little old man, who scoffed terribly at softness in any one, and who regarded himself as especial mastiff-in-waiting to protect the two young artists in the studio above.

Sue found Behrman smelling strongly of juniper berries[2] in his dimly lighted den below. In one corner was a blank canvas on an easel that had been waiting there for twenty-five years to receive the first line of the masterpiece. She told him of Johnsy's fancy, and how she feared she would, indeed, light and fragile as a leaf herself, float away when her slight hold upon the world grew weaker.

Old Behrman, with his red eyes plainly streaming, shouted his contempt and derision for such idiotic imaginings.

"Vass!" he cried. "Is dere people in de world mit der foolishness to die because leafs dey drop off from a confounded vine? I haf not heard of such a thing. No, I vill not bose as a model for your fool hermit-dunderhead. Vy do you allow dot silly business to come in der brain of her? Ach, dot poor lettle Miss Yohnsy."

"She is very ill and weak," said Sue, "and the fever has left her mind morbid and full of strange fancies. Very well, Mr. Behrman, if you do not care to pose for me, you needn't. But I think you are a horrid old—old flibbertigibbet."

"You are just like a woman!" yelled Behrman. "Who said I vill not bose? Go on. I come mit you. For half an hour I haf peen trying to say dot I am ready to bose. Gott! Dis is not any blace in which one so goot as Miss Yohnsy shall lie sick. Some day I vill baint a masterpiece, and ve shall all go avay. Gott! yes."

2. **juniper berries**—i.e., smelling of gin.

"The Last Leaf" by O. Henry

Stop and Organize

Make some notes in the "Characters" and "Dialogue" sections of the Synthesizing Chart on page 117.

Johnsy was sleeping when they went upstairs. Sue pulled the shade down to the window-sill, and motioned Behrman into the other room. In there they peered out the window fearfully at the ivy vine. Then they looked at each other for a moment without speaking. A persistent, cold rain was falling, mingled with snow. Behrman, in his old blue shirt, took his seat as the hermit-miner on an upturned kettle for a rock.

When Sue awoke from an hour's sleep the next morning she found Johnsy, with dull, wide-open eyes staring at the drawn green shade.

"Pull it up; I want to see," she ordered in a whisper.

Wearily Sue obeyed. But lo! after the beating rain and fierce gusts of wind that had endured through the livelong night, there yet stood out against the brick wall one ivy leaf. It was the last on the vine. Still dark-green near its stem, but with its serrated edges tinted with the yellow of dissolution and decay, it hung bravely from a branch some twenty feet above the ground.

"It is the last one," said Johnsy. "I thought it would surely fall during the night. I heard the wind. It will fall to-day, and I shall die at the same time."

"Dear, dear!" said Sue, leaning her worn face down to the pillow; "think of me, if you won't think of yourself. What would I do?"

But Johnsy did not answer. The lonesomest thing in all the world is a soul when it is making ready to go on its mysterious, far journey. The fancy seemed to possess her more strongly as one by one the ties that bound her to friendship and to earth were loosed.

The day wore away, and even through the twilight they could see the lone ivy leaf clinging to its stem against the wall. And then, with the coming of the night the north wind was again loosed, while the rain still beat against the windows and pattered down from the low Dutch eaves.

When it was light enough Johnsy, the merciless, commanded that the shade be raised.

The ivy leaf was still there.

Johnsy lay for a long time looking at it. And then she called to Sue, who was stirring her chicken broth over the gas stove.

"I've been a bad girl, Sudie," said Johnsy. "Something has made that last leaf stay there to show me how wicked I was. It is a sin to want to die. You may bring me a little broth now, and some milk with a little port in it, and no; bring me a hand-mirror first; and then pack some pillows about me, and I will sit up and watch you cook."

An hour later she said "Sudie, some day I hope to paint the Bay of Naples."

Fiction

NAME ....

FOR USE WITH PAGES 267–287

"The Last Leaf" by O. Henry

The doctor came in the afternoon, and Sue had an excuse to go into the hallway as he left.

"Even chances," said the doctor, taking Sue's thin, shaking hand in his. "With good nursing you'll win. And now I must see another case I have downstairs. Behrman, he is some kind of an artist, I believe. Pneumonia, too. He is an old, weak man, and the attack is acute. There is no hope for him; but he goes to the hospital to-day to be made more comfortable."

The next day the doctor said to Sue: "She's out of danger. You've won. Nutrition and care now that's all."

And that afternoon Sue came to the bed where Johnsy lay contentedly knitting a very blue and very useless woolen shoulder scarf, and put one arm around her, pillows and all.

"I have something to tell you, white mouse," she said. "Mr. Behrman died of pneumonia to-day in the hospital. He was ill only two days. The janitor found him on the morning of the first day in his room downstairs helpless with pain. His shoes and clothing were wet through and icy cold. They couldn't imagine where he had been on such a dreadful night. And then they found a lantern, still lighted, and a ladder that had been dragged from its place and some scattered brushes, and a palette with green and yellow colors mixed on it, and look out the window, dear, at the last ivy leaf on the wall. Didn't you wonder why it never fluttered or moved when the wind blew? Ah, darling, it's Behrman's masterpiece—he painted it there the night that the last leaf fell."

Stop and Organize

Make some notes in the "Plot" section of the Synthesizing Chart on page 117.

C Plan

Next, choose a strategy that can help you meet your purpose.

• **Practice the strategy of synthesizing.**

When you synthesize, you look at a number of elements and pull them together to form a new product.

During Reading

D Read with a Purpose

Directions: Do a careful reading of "The Last Leaf." Write your notes on this organizer. If you need help, see pages 277–279 of the *Reader's Handbook*.

Synthesizing Chart

Write facts from the story here.	Write your thoughts or the most important thoughts here.
Characters Sue, Johnsy, Mr. Behrman They are all "starving" artists living in New York.	Sue, Johnsy, and Mr. Behrman all think it's possible to will yourself to die. I don't think that can really happen.
Setting Greenwich Village in New York City. It is fall. I can tell the story took place a long time ago because of the way the characters and narrator talk.	The time of the year—fall—is really important. It explains why the vine is shedding its leaves.
Plot Johnsy has pneumonia. She is so sick that she thinks she will die when the last leaf from a vine outside the window falls. Sue and Mr. Behrman are determined that she will live.	I liked the surprise ending! I figured Johnsy would die as soon as she saw that the last leaf was down.
Dialogue The two girls say affectionate things to each other and call each other pet names. Mr. Behrman speaks with a German accent that is hard to understand.	I noticed that Mr. Behrman sounds mad when he talks. This makes the surprise at the end all the more surprising. You don't expect something like this from him.
Theme I think the author is saying that the greatest thing you can do is to help someone else. Helping Johnsy ends up being Behrman's masterpiece.	I agree with this idea that an act of kindness can be someone's masterpiece. More people should feel this way.

Fiction

Using the Strategy

There are many different types of reading tools that can help you synthesize the elements in a story.

• **A Story Organizer will help you reflect on the plot of a story.**

Directions: Make notes about the plot and theme of "The Last Leaf" on the Story Organizer below.

Story Organizer

Beginning	Middle	End
Johnsy catches pneumonia and thinks that she will die when the last leaf falls from the vine outside her window.	Sue tells Mr. Behrman about Johnsy. Behrman comes up to their studio and sees how sick Johnsy is.	Johnsy awakens, sees that the last leaf remains, and decides to live. Sue admits that Behrman painted the leaf to trick Johnsy.

Possible Theme: Helping someone else can be your own personal "masterpiece."

Understanding How Short Stories Are Organized

A short story's plot can be divided into five basic parts: exposition, rising action, climax, falling action, and resolution.

Directions: Use the Plot Diagram on the next page to show the organization of "The Last Leaf." See page 280 of the *Reader's Handbook* if you need help.

NAME ....

FOR USE WITH PAGES 267–287

◀ **Plot Diagram**

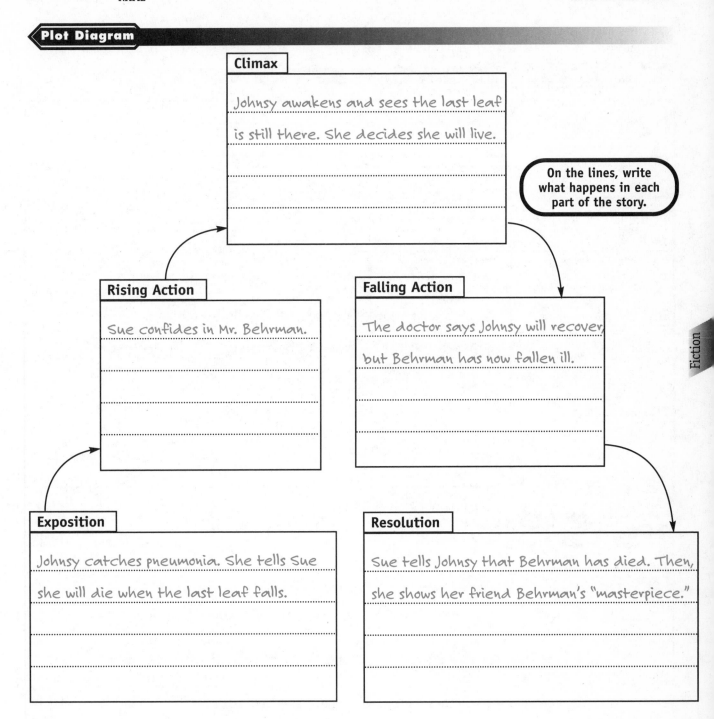

Climax

Johnsy awakens and sees the last leaf

is still there. She decides she will live.

On the lines, write
what happens in each
part of the story.

Fiction

Rising Action

Sue confides in Mr. Behrman.

Falling Action

The doctor says Johnsy will recover,

but Behrman has now fallen ill.

Exposition

Johnsy catches pneumonia. She tells Sue

she will die when the last leaf falls.

Resolution

Sue tells Johnsy that Behrman has died. Then,

she shows her friend Behrman's "masterpiece."

E **Connect**

You'll remember and enjoy a short story better if you connect it to your
own life.

- **Use a Making Connections Chart to think through your feelings about
  a story.**

Directions: Complete this chart for "The Last Leaf."

Making Connections Chart

I wonder why . . .	Johnsy made the connection between the last leaf falling and her dying. The author never explains it.
I think . . .	Johnsy is sort of a wimp. She doesn't fight to live.
This is similar to . . .	"The Gift of the Magi"—that story is also about making sacrifices and being selfless. That's how Behrman is in "The Last Leaf."
This reminds me of . . .	a friend who says that her grandmother and grandfather died just two weeks apart. She says they just couldn't live without each other.

After Reading

F Pause and Reflect

It is important when you finish a short story to reflect on the meaning. A good first step is to think about the ending.

- **After you finish a story, ask yourself, "Did things turn out the way I expected?"**

Directions: Answer these questions about "The Last Leaf."

How did you feel when you read the ending of "The Last Leaf"? I felt surprised.

Why did you feel this way? I expected Johnsy would die. I never thought Behrman would be of any help because he seemed sort of silly and useless, but he turned out to be a hero.

NAME

 Reread

When you reread, you notice things you missed the first time around. This will sharpen your understanding of the story.

• A good rereading strategy to use with short stories is close reading.

<u>Directions:</u> Read the quotations at the left of the organizer below. Skim the story to find where the quote appears. Then respond to each quote.

Close Reading Organizer

Text from "The Last Leaf"	What I Think about It
"Paint? Bosh! Has she anything on her mind worth thinking about twice—a man, for instance?"	This guy is a chauvinist! This kind of comment was typical for the time, but the doctor is not much help at all.
"Johnsy, dear," said Sue, bending over her, "will you promise me to keep your eyes closed, and not look out the window until I am done working?"	Sue is really worried about Johnsy. Could she have done more to help than tell Johnsy not to look out the window?
For the rest he was a fierce little old man, who scoffed terribly at softness in any one, and who regarded himself as especial mastiff-in-waiting to protect the two young artists in the studio above.	I didn't notice this on the first reading. He thinks of himself as a guard dog for Johnsy and Sue.
Behrman was a failure in art.	He proves his talent when he paints the last leaf.
"Ah, darling, it's Behrman's masterpiece—he painted it there the night that the last leaf fell."	He's no longer a failure. He has created a masterpiece.

Fiction

H **Remember**

Sharing a story can help you remember it. It can also sharpen your comprehension of the most important ideas.

- **To help you remember a story, discuss key aspects of the plot, characters, and theme.**

<u>Directions:</u> Get together in a small group to discuss "The Last Leaf." Use the prompts below, as well as one of your own that you've written beforehand, to stimulate a discussion of the short story. Write your discussion notes on the lines.

Discussion Prompts

What inferences can you make about Johnsy? about Sue? about Behrman?	**How is the leaf Behrman's masterpiece?**
Johnsy is sort of wimpy and silly. It's dumb that she just lies there and waits for the leaf to fall. Sue is not much better. She just kind of stands by and waits for the leaf to drop. But Behrman is brave enough and smart enough to take matters into his own hands.	Behrman spent his whole life hoping to paint a masterpiece. When he learned that Johnsy was willing herself to die as soon as the last leaf fell from the vine, he decided to paint the leaf onto the wall. In doing so, he saves Johnsy's life. This is why Sue calls the leaf painting a masterpiece.
Which character do you think was the most responsible for Johnsy's recovery? Why?	**How would the story be different if it were told from Behrman's point of view?**
I think it was Behrman. He actually did something to help Johnsy.	If the story had been told from Behrman's point of view, the surprise ending would have been lost. We would know all along what Behrman was planning.

My discussion question: What is O. Henry's theme in "The Last Leaf"?

O. Henry wants us to think about will power, hope, and sacrifice. The theme is that we can make a difference.

Reading a Novel

Reading a novel is like taking a long and mysterious journey. The reading process is a road map you can use to keep from getting lost. It will can also help you understand and enjoy the people, places, and things you see along the way.

Before Reading

Here, you'll practice using the reading process with an excerpt from the novel *Great Expectations* by Charles Dickens.

 Set a Purpose

Your primary purpose for reading a novel is enjoyment. But if you're reading the book for school, it will be important to recognize and remember the novel's point of view, characters, setting, plot, and theme.

• **To set your purpose, ask important questions about the major literary elements of the novel.**

Directions: You will be reading Chapter 1 of *Great Expectations*. Write your purpose questions on the chart below. (The first one is done for you.)

Purpose Chart

Element	My Questions
point of view	From whose perspective is the story told?
characters	Who are the major characters?
setting	Where and when does the story take place?
plot	What happens to the characters in this chapter of the story?
theme	What are the themes that have appeared?

Fiction

B Preview

Always spend a moment or two previewing the novel you're about to read. Begin by examining the front and back covers of the book.

Directions: Preview the front and back covers of *Great Expectations*. Write important facts and details on the sticky notes.

Back Cover

Within these pages find Charles Dickens's tale of Pip's coming of age— one of the most widely read novels of all time.

First published in 1861, *Great Expectations* is the story of a young orphan who travels the gloomy graveyards, damp marshlands, and bustling city streets of Victorian England in search of home and happiness. Along the way, he meets a half-mad spinster, a vicious young woman whose beauty is a weapon, and an escaped convict who carries with him a secret that threatens to bring heartbreak and ruin to everyone Pip has ever known.

Front Cover

GREAT EXPECTATIONS

by Charles Dickens

Important information about the book: It is the story of an orphan named Pip who longs for a home and happiness. The book was first published in 1861.

Details that relate to my purpose: The setting is Victorian England. The central character is Pip, and there are at least three other characters.

The title: Great Expectations
The author: Charles Dickens

NAME

 Plan

After your preview, choose a strategy that can help you respond to the novel.

• Good readers know that using graphic organizers can help them get more from a novel.

Directions: Look over the Fiction Organizer so that you will know ahead of time what to pay attention to as you read Chapter 1 of *Great Expectations*.

◄ Fiction Organizer

Point of View The story is told from Pip's point of view. He is the "I" of the story.

Characters Pip and a frightening-looking man

Charles Dickens, *Great Expectations*

Setting The novel takes place in Victorian England. This chapter is set in a graveyard near Pip's house.

Plot A stranger approaches Pip in a graveyard. He tells Pip to bring him some food and a file. Pip is scared.

Theme I think misfortune or being unlucky might be a big idea in this book. There might also be something about fear or learning to be brave.

Fiction

During Reading

D Read with a Purpose

Completing a Fiction Organizer as you read can make it easier to stay focused on your purpose.

Directions: Now, do a careful reading of Chapter 1 of *Great Expectations*. As you read, think about point of view, the characters, setting, plot, and theme.

> **from *Great Expectations* by Charles Dickens**

My father's family name being Pirrip, and my Christian name Philip, my infant tongue could make of both names nothing longer or more explicit than Pip. So, I called myself Pip, and came to be called Pip.

I give Pirrip as my father's family name, on the authority of his tombstone and my sister—Mrs. Joe Gargery, who married the blacksmith. As I never saw my father or my mother, and never saw any likeness of either of them (for their days were long before the days of photographs), my first fancies regarding what they were like, were unreasonably derived from their tombstones. The shape of the letters on my father's, gave me an odd idea that he was a square, stout, dark man, with curly black hair. From the character and turn of the inscription, *"Also Georgiana Wife of the Above,"* I drew a childish conclusion that my mother was freckled and sickly. To five little stone lozenges, each about a foot and a half long, which were arranged in a neat row beside their grave, and were sacred to the memory of five little brothers of mine—who gave up trying to get a living exceedingly early in that universal struggle—I am indebted for a belief I religiously entertained that they had all been born on their backs with their hands in their trousers-pockets, and had never taken them out in this state of existence.

Ours was the marsh country, down by the river, within, as the river wound, twenty miles of the sea. My first most vivid and broad impression of the identity of things, seems to me to have been gained on a memorable raw afternoon towards evening. At such a time I found out for certain, that this bleak place overgrown with nettles was the churchyard; and that Philip Pirrip, late of this parish, and also Georgiana wife of the above, were dead and buried; and that Alexander, Bartholomew, Abraham, Tobias, and Roger, infant children of the aforesaid, were also dead and buried; and that the dark flat wilderness beyond the churchyard, intersected with dykes and mounds and gates, with scattered cattle feeding on it, was the marshes; and that the low leaden line beyond, was the river; and that the distant savage lair from which the wind was rushing, was the sea; and that the small bundle of shivers growing afraid of it all and beginning to cry, was Pip.

Stop and Organize

What is the story's setting? From whose point of view is the story told? Make notes on the Fiction Organizer on page 125.

from *Great Expectations* by Charles Dickens

"Hold your noise!" cried a terrible voice, as a man started up from among the graves at the side of the church porch. "Keep still, you little devil, or I'll cut your throat!"

A fearful man, all in coarse grey, with a great iron on his leg. A man with no hat, and with broken shoes, and with an old rag tied round his head. A man who had been soaked in water, and smothered in mud, and lamed by stones, and cut by flints, and stung by nettles, and torn by briars; who limped, and shivered, and glared and growled; and whose teeth chattered in his head as he seized me by the chin.

"O! Don't cut my throat, sir," I pleaded in terror. "Pray don't do it, sir."

"Tell us your name!" said the man. "Quick!"

"Pip, sir."

"Once more," said the man, staring at me. "Give it mouth!"

"Pip. Pip, sir."

"Show us where you live," said the man. "Pint out the place!"

I pointed to where our village lay, on the flat in-shore among the alder-trees and pollards, a mile or more from the church.

The man, after looking at me for a moment, turned me upside down, and emptied my pockets. There was nothing in them but a piece of bread. When the church came to itself—for he was so sudden and strong that he made it go head over heels before me, and I saw the steeple under my feet—when the church came to itself, I say, I was seated on a high tombstone, trembling, while he ate the bread ravenously.

"You young dog," said the man, licking his lips, "what fat cheeks you ha' got."

I believe they were fat, though I was at that time undersized for my years, and not strong.

"Darn me if I couldn't eat em," said the man, with a threatening shake of his head, "and if I han't half a mind to't!"

I earnestly expressed my hope that he wouldn't, and held tighter to the tombstone on which he had put me; partly, to keep myself upon it; partly, to keep myself from crying.

"Now lookee here!" said the man. "Where's your mother?"

"There, sir!" said I.

He started, made a short run, and stopped and looked over his shoulder.

"There, sir!" I timidly explained. "Also Georgiana. That's my mother."

"Oh!" said he, coming back. "And is that your father alonger your mother?"

"Yes, sir," said I; "him too; late of this parish."

"Ha!" he muttered then, considering. "Who d'ye live with—supposin' you're kindly let to live, which I han't made up my mind about?"

"My sister, sir—Mrs. Joe Gargery—wife of Joe Gargery, the blacksmith, sir."

"Blacksmith, eh?" said he. And looked down at his leg.

After darkly looking at his leg and me several times, he came closer to my tombstone, took me by both arms, and tilted me back as far as he could hold me; so that his eyes looked most powerfully down into mine, and mine looked most helplessly up into his.

◁ from *Great Expectations* by Charles Dickens ▷

"Now lookee here," he said, "the question being whether you're to be let to live. You know what a file is?"

"Yes, sir."

"And you know what wittles is?"

"Yes, sir."

After each question he tilted me over a little more, so as to give me a greater sense of helplessness and danger.

"You get me a file." He tilted me again. "And you get me wittles." He tilted me again. "You bring 'em both to me." He tilted me again. "Or I'll have your heart and liver out." He tilted me again.

Stop and Organize

What inferences can you make about Pip? What inferences can you make about the stranger? Make notes on the Fiction Organizer on page 125.

I was dreadfully frightened, and so giddy that I clung to him with both hands, and said, "If you would kindly please to let me keep upright, sir, perhaps I shouldn't be sick, and perhaps I could attend more."

He gave me a most tremendous dip and roll, so that the church jumped over its own weather-cock. Then, he held me by the arms, in an upright position on the top of the stone, and went on in these fearful terms:

"You bring me, to-morrow morning early, that file and them wittles. You bring the lot to me, at that old Battery over yonder. You do it, and you never dare to say a word or dare to make a sign concerning your having seen such a person as me, or any person sumever, and you shall be let to live. You fail, or you go from my words in any partickler, no matter how small it is, and your heart and your liver shall be tore out, roasted and ate. Now, I ain't alone, as you may think I am. There's a young man hid with me, in comparison with which young man I am a Angel. That young man hears the words I speak. That young man has a secret way pecooliar to himself, of getting at a boy, and at his heart, and at his liver. It is in wain for a boy to attempt to hide himself from that young man. A boy may lock his door, may be warm in bed, may tuck himself up, may draw the clothes over his head, may think himself comfortable and safe, but that young man will softly creep and creep his way to him and tear him open. I am a-keeping that young man from harming of you at the present moment, with great difficulty. I find it wery hard to hold that young man off of your inside. Now, what do you say?"

Stop and Organize

What would you say are some of the big ideas or possible themes in this novel? Make notes on the Fiction Organizer on page 125.

from *Great Expectations* by Charles Dickens

I said that I would get him the file, and I would get him what broken bits of food I could, and I would come to him at the Battery, early in the morning.

"Say, Lord strike you dead if you don't!" said the man.

I said so, and he took me down.

"Now," he pursued, "you remember what you've undertook, and you remember that young man, and you get home!"

"Goo-good night, sir," I faltered.

"Much of that!" said he, glancing about him over the cold wet flat. "I wish I was a frog. Or a eel!"

At the same time, he hugged his shuddering body in both his arms—clasping himself, as if to hold himself together—and limped towards the low church wall. As I saw him go, picking his way among the nettles, and among the brambles that bound the green mounds, he looked in my young eyes as if he were eluding the hands of the dead people, stretching up cautiously out of their graves, to get a twist upon his ankle and pull him in.

When he came to the low church wall, he got over it, like a man whose legs were numbed and stiff, and then turned round to look for me. When I saw him turning, I set my face towards home, and made the best use of my legs. But presently I looked over my shoulder, and saw him going on again towards the river, still hugging himself in both arms, and picking his way with his sore feet among the great stones dropped into the marshes here and there, for stepping-places when the rains were heavy, or the tide was in.

The marshes were just a long black horizontal line then, as I stopped to look after him; and the river was just another horizontal line, not nearly so broad nor yet so black; and the sky was just a row of long angry red lines and dense black lines intermixed. On the edge of the river I could faintly make out the only two black things in all the prospect that seemed to be standing upright; one of these was the beacon by which the sailors steered—like an unhooped cask upon a pole—an ugly thing when you were near it; the other a gibbet, with some chains hanging to it which had once held a pirate. The man was limping on towards this latter, as if he were the pirate come to life, and come down, and going back to hook himself up again. It gave me a terrible turn when I thought so; and as I saw the cattle lifting their heads to gaze after him, I wondered whether they thought so too. I looked all round for the horrible young man, and could see no signs of him. But, now I was frightened again, and ran home without stopping.

Stop and Organize

What happens in this chapter of the book? What are the key events? Make notes on the Fiction Organizer on page 125.

Fiction

Using the Strategy

There are all kinds of graphic organizers that you can use with a novel. A Character Map is a good one to use at the beginning of a novel to help you get to know the book's main character.

Directions: Make notes about Pip on this Character Map.

Character Map

How he looks: Fat cheeks, undersized for his years

How he acts, what he says: He is frightened and begs the stranger to be good to him. He promises he'll bring the man anything he wants.

What he thinks, feels: At the beginning, he's feeling sad about his family. When the stranger comes, he starts to worry that something will happen to him.

Pip

How others react to him: The stranger takes advantage of Pip because he's young. He turns him upside down, threatens him, and tells him to bring him food and a file.

What I've learned about him so far: He's pretty young and doesn't have much confidence of his own. But he's polite and wants to help.

Understanding How Novels Are Organized

The plots of most novels are in chronological order. A graphic organizer will help you keep track of what is happening.

• A Story String can help you see how one event leads to another.

Directions: Think about what happens in Chapter 1 of *Great Expectations*. Then, make notes on this Story String.

Story String

Pip stares at his family's graves in the graveyard.

A terrible-looking man grabs him and steals his bread.

The man shakes Pip and demands food and a file.

Pip swears he will do as he is told.

Pip runs off in the direction of home.

E Connect

You can't help but react to the characters and events in a novel. Keeping track of your reactions will help you make sense of a novel.

- **Making connections with a novel means recording your thoughts and feelings about the text.**

Directions: Read the quotes from *Great Expectations* on the left of the Double-entry Journal below. Write how they make you feel or what they remind you of on the right.

Double-Entry Journal

Quotes	My Reactions
A man who had been soaked in water, and smothered in mud, and lamed by stones, and cut by flints, and stung by nettles, and torn by briars; who limped, and shivered, and glared and growled; and whose teeth chattered in his head as he seized me by the chin.	This guy is really a mess. I wonder if this is the escaped convict I read about on the back cover?
I was dreadfully frightened, and so giddy that I clung to him with both hands, and said, "If you would kindly please to let me keep upright, sir, perhaps I shouldn't be sick, and perhaps I could attend more."	I think this is kind of funny. Pip is more worried about his dizziness than anything else.

After Reading

When you finish reading, it is important to take a moment or two to think about your purpose.

F Pause and Reflect

Keep in mind that your purpose was to find details about point of view, the characters, setting, plot, and theme.

- **After you finish a novel, ask yourself, "How well did I meet my purpose?"**

Fiction

131

Directions: Answer these questions about the chapter you just read from
Great Expectations.

▶ **Looking Back**

Question	My Answer	What I Need to Understand Better
Do I know the point of view?	(yes) no	What sort of person Pip is.
Do I have a strong understanding of the characters I've met thus far?	(yes) no	What sort of person the convict is
Can I visualize the setting?	(yes) no	What time of year it is
Do I understand the plot up to this point?	(yes) no	I'd like a better sense of Pip's feelings about being an orphan.
Have I begun to think about the big ideas or themes in the work?	yes (no)	I need to go back and reconsider what the "frightful man" may represent.

 Reread

If you haven't met your purpose, you may need to do some rereading.
Rather than reread word-for-word, however, you'll want to skim chunks of
the novel for clues about one of the major literary elements. The rereading
strategy of synthesizing can help.

- **Use synthesizing to help you see how the parts of a novel fit
  together.**

Directions: Complete this synthesizing chart for Chapter 1 of *Great Expectations*. If you need help, see page 279 of the *Reader's Handbook*.

◄ **Synthesizing Chart**

Great Expectations, Chapter 1	What I Think
Characters The characters are Pip and a stranger. Pip is a young orphan who visits the graveyard where his parents are buried because he's lonely. The stranger is a terrible-looking man who "growls" instead of talks.	Pip is meek and the stranger is fierce. They are exact opposites.
Setting A graveyard on a marsh in England. It is damp and cold and really nasty out.	The gloomy setting makes the novel seem like it might be a scary one.
Plot A stranger grabs Pip, who is sitting by himself in a graveyard. The stranger threatens to kill Pip if Pip doesn't bring him food and a file.	I guess the stranger is going to use the file to cut the iron off his leg. I'm picturing a ball and chain, like the kind a convict wore in olden times.
Theme A big idea in this book might be misfortune.	An example of misfortune is the fact that Pip was very unlucky to be at the graveyard at the exact moment the convict comes up. I'll need to read more to find out if this idea turns into an actual theme.

Fiction

Remember

It's important to remember what happens from one chapter to another in a novel.

- **Writing a brief summary of each chapter will help you keep track of what happens in a novel.**

Directions: Write a brief summary of Chapter 1 of *Great Expectations*.

Summary

Great Expectations

Chapter 1

The scene opens in a graveyard. Pip is looking at the graves of his family, as he often does. He is interrupted by a stranger who is dressed in rags and has an iron around his leg. Pip is terrified. The stranger asks Pip to identify himself and then demands that the boy run home and fetch some food and a file. A terrified Pip agrees to do as the stranger asks. He runs off toward home and leaves the stranger in the graveyard.

Focus on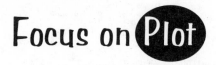

Plot is the arrangement of events in a work of fiction. In this lesson, you'll explore the plot of a Greek myth.

Step 1 Track the key events.

On your first reading of a story, keep an eye on what happens in the plot.

Directions: Read this myth about Pandora. Underline key events in the plot. Make any notes on the stickies.

"Pandora" by Edith Hamilton

Another story about Pandora is that the source of all misfortune was not her wicked nature, but only her curiosity. The <u>gods presented her with a box</u> into which each had put something harmful, and forbade her to ever open it. Then they <u>sent her to Epimetheus</u>, who took her gladly although Prometheus had warned him never to accept anything from Zeus. He took her, and afterward when that dangerous thing, a woman, was his, he understood how good his brother's advice had been. For Pandora *had* to know what was in the box. One day she <u>lifted the lid—and out flew plagues innumerable, sorrow, and mischief for mankind</u>. In terror <u>Pandora clapped the lid down</u>, but too late. One good thing, however, was there—Hope. It was the only good the casket had held among the many evils, and it remains to this day mankind's sole comfort in misfortune.

1. Gods give Pandora a box.
2. Gods give Pandora to Epimetheus.
3. Pandora opens the box.
4. Innumerable sorrow and plagues are released.

Why was hope in the box of bad things?

Step 2 Diagram the plot.

Now that you've read the myth, describe the five parts of the plot—
exposition, rising action, climax, falling action, and resolution—on a
Plot Diagram.

Directions: Complete this Plot Diagram using key events from "Pandora."

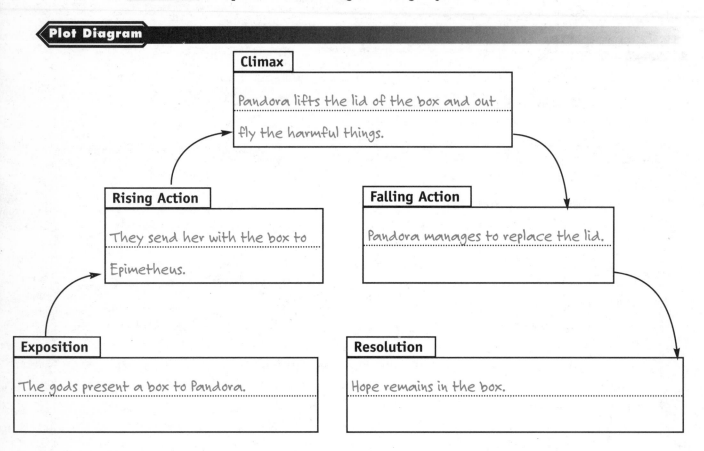

Plot Diagram

Climax

Pandora lifts the lid of the box and out fly the harmful things.

Rising Action

They send her with the box to Epimetheus.

Falling Action

Pandora manages to replace the lid.

Exposition

The gods present a box to Pandora.

Resolution

Hope remains in the box.

Step 3 Consider the climax.

The climax is the turning point in the action of a story.

Directions: Reread what you wrote on your Plot Diagram. Then, explain the
point at which the climax occurs in "Pandora."

In "Pandora," the climax occurs when Pandora slides the lid off the box and

lets all these horrible things out. This is the turning point in the action.

_____

_____

Focus on Setting

The setting affects the mood, characters, and plot of a story.

Step 1 Do a close reading.

As you read, carefully note the details of the story's setting. You usually can infer a great deal from them.

Directions: Read this paragraph. Underline any clues about time and place.

---

from *The House of Sand and Fog* by Andre Dubus III

The fat one he calls me because I am Persian and because I can bear this August sun longer than the Chinese and the Panamanians and even the little Vietnamese, Tran. He works very quickly without rest, but when Torez stops the orange highway truck in front of the crew, Tran hurries for his paper cup of water with the rest of them. This heat is no good for work. All morning we have walked this highway between Sausalito and the Golden Gate Park. We carry our small trash harpoons and we drag our burlap bags and we are dressed in vests the same color as the highway truck. Some of the Panamanians remove their shirts and leave them hanging from their back pockets like oil rags, but Torez says something to them in their mother language and he makes them wear the vests over their bare backs. We are up on a small hill. Between the trees I can see out over Sausalito to the bay where there are clouds so thick I cannot see the other side where I live with my family in Berkeley, my wife and son. But here there is no fog, only sun on your head and back, and the smell of everything under the nose: the dry grass and dirt; the cigarette smoke of the Chinese; the hot metal and exhaust of the passing automobiles. ...

Fiction

Step 2 Draw conclusions about mood and character.

The setting of a story can make you feel a certain way or give you ideas about the characters. In other words, it can affect both mood and characterization.

Directions: Read these details about the setting. Then, write your inferences about mood and character.

Inference Chart

Quotes from the Text	My Thoughts about Mood	My Thoughts about Character
I can bear this August sun longer	All that broiling heat. There is a feeling of growing tension in this paragraph, as if something is coming. By the end of the paragraph, everyone is completely miserable, including the narrator.	The narrator is bothered by the heat, but not as much as the others. He's not a complainer. He kind of accepts the dry landscape for what it is.
All morning we have walked this highway	The main character and his group are working hard at a monotonous task. It adds to the closeness of the mood.	He works hard and does not seem a part of the group, perhaps because he is from a different country.
But here there is no fog, only sun on your head and back	The narrator's vision is limited. He seems trapped by the weather and environment.	He seems to long for home. He wants to see something that can carry his mind away from the heat and work.

Step 3 Make predictions.

The descriptions of the setting can help you understand the plot of a story. It will give you clues about what's to come.

Directions: Make a prediction about what you think happens next in *The House of Sand and Fog*. Then, describe how you made your prediction.

My prediction: I think tempers are running high because of the heat and the horrible work on the highway. I predict that these men will get into a fight or do something bad. That's what can happen when people are really hot and tired.

My reasoning: The author is using the characters' various reactions to the heat to set up who they are and how they will relate. The heat dominates the setting. It seems like the summer is going to be a big part of the story.

Fiction

FOR USE WITH PAGES 332–344

Focus on Characters

Some stories are more memorable for the characters than anything else. A powerful main character can drive the action and shape the themes of an entire work.

Step 1 Read for character clues.

Directions: Read this excerpt from a novel about a teenager named Sean who has been unable to voluntarily move a muscle since birth. Make notes about Sean on the sticky.

from *Stuck in Neutral* by Terry Trueman

Nobody has ever said to me, "Blink your eyes twice if you understand me," or tried to teach me Morse code so that if I could control my neck muscles I might bang out something like "Howdy, I remember everything I hear so would you mind playing a little rock and roll?" Nobody has ever held my fingers over a Ouija board or drawn letters with their fingers on my chest. Nobody's ever tried any of these Hollywood-movie techniques of making contact. They think I'm too far gone for that. But the fact is none of these things would work anyhow. They wouldn't work for me because I can't control *any* of my muscles; I've never been able to and I know that I never will. My brain just can't do it. Period. "Blink your eyes if you understand." Well, if I could, I would. I'm trying, like I've tried ten million times before, and it doesn't work; I can't control my blinks. "Bounce your head if you want some chocolate cake." I'd love some chocolate cake, but not only can I not bounce my head, I can't even chew the cake if you shove some into my mouth. I have to just let it sit there and kind of melt into chocolate mush and wait for my swallow reflex to kick in.

What I know about Sean: He's paralyzed. He can't voluntarily move any muscles. No one tries to make contact with him because they assume he doesn't know what's going on. But he's actually very aware.

Step 2 Make inferences.

Now, use the clues you've found to help you make inferences about
the character.

Directions: Complete this inference chart about Sean.

◄ **Inference Chart**

The Character's Thoughts	What I Can Conclude about Him
"Howdy, I remember everything I hear so would you mind playing a little rock and roll?"	He's got a good sense of humor. He's aware of everything around him and wishes he could tell everyone.
They think I'm too far gone for that.	He is really aware of what's going on around him, and I think he might be kind of frustrated by the fact that he can't do what others do.
Well, if I could, I would. I'm trying, like I've tried ten million times before, and it doesn't work, I can't control my blinks.	He's no quitter. He wants to make contact, but he can't.

Step 3 Connect character to theme.

Remember that a character's thoughts and actions can often point the way
to important themes in the work.

Directions: A big idea in *Stuck in Neutral* is "facing adversity." Make a
connection between this idea and the character of Sean. Write your ideas on
the lines.

Big idea: Facing adversity

My ideas: Sean has bigger problems than anyone I've ever read about. He can't voluntarily
move any muscles. This is adversity in the extreme. But he's pretty matter-of-fact about his
problems. From the way he "talks," you can tell that he doesn't just sit and dwell on what's
wrong with his life. This is an example of facing adversity in a really positive way.

Focus on Theme

Remember that themes are the statements about life that the author wants to convey in a story. You will find clues about themes by examining the plot and characters of a story.

Step 1 Identify the "big ideas" or central topics.

To find the central topics of a story, ask yourself, "What people, places, and things is the author talking about?"

Directions: Reread "Pandora" (which you originally read on page 135). Then write three of the myth's central topics below.

"Pandora" by Edith Hamilton

Another story about Pandora is that the source of all misfortune was not her wicked nature, but only her curiosity. The gods presented her with a box into which each had put something harmful, and forbade her to ever open it. Then they sent her to Epimetheus, who took her gladly although Prometheus had warned him never to accept anything from Zeus. He took her, and afterward when that dangerous thing, a woman, was his, he understood how good his brother's advice had been. For Pandora *had* to know what was in the box. One day she lifted the lid—and out flew plagues innumerable, sorrow, and mischief for mankind. In terror Pandora clapped the lid down, but too late. One good thing, however, was there—Hope. It was the only good the casket had held among the many evils, and it remains to this day mankind's sole comfort in misfortune....

Central Topics

Topic #1	Topic #2	Topic #3
misfortune	curiosity	hope

Step 2 Consider what the characters do and say.

Next, make a connection between the topics and the characters in the work.

Directions: Read the following quotes from "Pandora." Then explain how they relate to the big ideas in the myth.

Inference Chart

Quote	What I Think about It
Another story about Pandora is that the source of all misfortune was not her wicked nature, but only her curiosity.	This relates to the idea that curiosity is bad. Pandora created her own troubles.
One day she lifted the lid—and out flew plagues innumerable, sorrow, and mischief for mankind.	Pandora is showing her curiosity here. She can't stop herself from lifting the lid. As a result, all kinds of bad things will now happen.
It was the only good the casket had held among the many evils, and it remains to this day mankind's sole comfort in misfortune.	The only thing good is Hope. The line means that no matter what misfortune comes your way, you still have hope that things will improve.

Step 3 **Think about the point the author is making.**

The theme is the point the author is making about the central topic. When trying to figure out the theme of a work you have just read, try this formula:

Central Idea + What the Author Says About the Central Topic = The Theme of the Work

Directions: Use the formula to help you find one theme in "Pandora."

......hope..

....+..

......it is important to humans..

....=..

......No matter what our misfortunes, we still have hope.................

Fiction

Step 4 Pull it all together.

After you identify a theme, you need to find details in the story that support it.

Directions: Explore the theme of "hope" in the myth "Pandora." Make notes on this Topic and Theme Organizer.

Topic and Theme Organizer

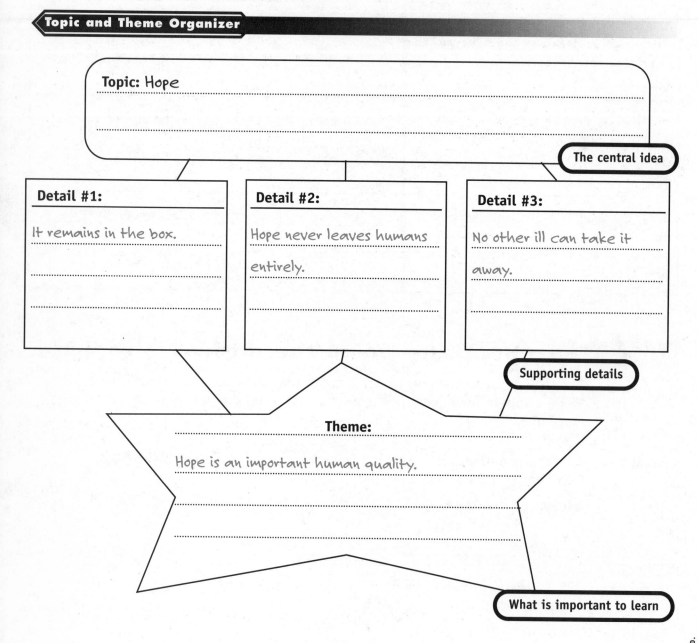

Topic: Hope

....

....

The central idea

Detail #1:

It remains in the box.

....

....

Detail #2:

Hope never leaves humans

entirely.

....

Detail #3:

No other ill can take it

away.

....

....

Supporting details

Theme:

Hope is an important human quality.

....

....

What is important to learn

Focus on Dialogue

One of an author's main tools for telling you what a character is like is dialogue. Listen carefully to what a character is saying, and you will learn a great deal about them.

Step 1 Do a close reading.

Use the strategy of close reading to help you "hear" what the characters are saying.

Directions: Carefully read this conversation between a mother and a daughter. Make notes on the stickies.

from "What Means Switch" by Gish Jen

...One day I say, "You know Ma, I have never seen a stir-fried tomato in any Chinese restaurant we have ever been in, ever."

"In China," she says, real lofty, "we consider tomatoes are a delicacy."

"Ma," I say. "Tomatoes are *Italian*."

"No respect for elders." She wags her finger at me, but I can tell it's just to try and shame me into believing her. "I'm tell you, tomatoes *invented* in China."

"*Ma*."

"Is true. Like noodles. Invented in China."

"That's not what they said in *school*."

"In *China*," my mother counters, "we also eat tomatoes uncooked, like apple. And in summertime we slice them, and put some sugar on top."

"Are you sure?"

My mom says of course she's sure, and in the end I give in, even though she once told me that China was such a long time ago, a lot of things she can hardly remember.

This conversation is
between a mother
and her daughter.

They are talking
about tomatoes and
whether or not the
mother really
remembers what
China was like.

This is how the characters sound:
The daughter sounds irritated and
makes it clear she does not believe
what her mother is saying. The mother
sounds bossy, like she's determined to
win this argument with her daughter.

Fiction

Step 2 Look for clues about character.

Next, make inferences about the characters based on what they said.

Directions: Write something each character says in the left column. Then, write your inferences about the character on the right.

Inference Chart

What the _daughter_ Says	My Inferences about the Character
"That's not what they said in school."	The daughter is irritated. She is challenging what her mother knows.

What the _mother_ Says	My Inferences about the Character
"No respect for elders."	The mother is criticizing the daughter for arguing. You sense that they've had arguments like this before, and that the mother insists on respect just because she is older.

Step 3 Look for clues about mood.

Dialogue also contributes to the mood of a story.

Directions: Reread the information about dialogue and mood on page 356 of the *Reader's Handbook*. Then, describe the mood of the scene from "What Means Switch."

I think the mood is tense   because the characters are arguing. Neither wants to give in

or admit that she is wrong.

....

....

....

....

....

Fiction

Step 4 Look for clues about plot.

Very often, dialogue can give you clues about what is going to happen next in a story.

Directions: Make a prediction of what will happen next in this story. Then explain your prediction.

My prediction: I think the daughter will give in and agree that her mother is right.

....

....

....

I think this will happen because: the mother is clearly not going to give up, and the daughter

seems resigned to letting her mother have her way.

....

....

....

....

....

....

Focus on Comparing and Contrasting

Comparing and contrasting how two writers use the same literary element is a very common exercise.

Step 1 Read and make notes.

When comparing and contrasting two works, you need to begin by reading them both carefully with the same questions in mind. Then, choose the element you want to compare and make some notes.

Directions: Read these novel excerpts. Make notes about the two characters—Francie, in the first, and Holden, the narrator of the second.

from *A Tree Grows in Brooklyn* by Betty Smith

Francie thought that all the books in the world were in that library and she had a plan about reading all the books in the world. She was reading a book a day in alphabetical order and not skipping the dry ones. She remembered that the first author had been Abbott. She had been reading a book a day for a long time now and she was still in the B's. Already she had read about bees and buffaloes, Bermuda vacations and Byzantine architecture. For all of her enthusiasm, she had to admit that some of the B's were hard going. But Francie was a reader. She read everything she could find: trash, classics, time tables and the grocer's price list. Some of the reading had been wonderful; the Louisa Alcott books for example. She planned to read all the books over again when she had finished with the Z's.

What I can infer about Francie:

She is intelligent and determined. She is also a little naïve to think that she can read every book in the library.

from *The Catcher in the Rye* by J. D. Salinger

Where I want to start telling is the day I left Pencey Prep. Pencey Prep is this school that's in Agerstown, Pennsylvania. You probably hear of it. You've probably seen the ads, anyway. They advertise in about a thousand magazines, always showing some hotshot guy on a horse jumping over a fence. Like as if all you ever did at Pencey was play polo all the time. I never even once saw a horse anywhere near the place. And underneath the guy on the horse's picture, it always says: "Since 1888 we have been molding boys into splendid, clear-thinking young men." Strictly for the birds. They don't do any damn more *molding* at Pencey than they do at any other school. And I didn't know anybody there that was splendid and clear-thinking at all. . . .

What I can infer about Holden:

He's clearly intelligent, but he's pretty sarcastic. He is very critical of his school.

NAME

Step 2 Organize.

Using graphic organizers can help you sort important details in the two works.

Directions: Compare Francie and Holden on this Venn Diagram.

◄ **Venn Diagram**

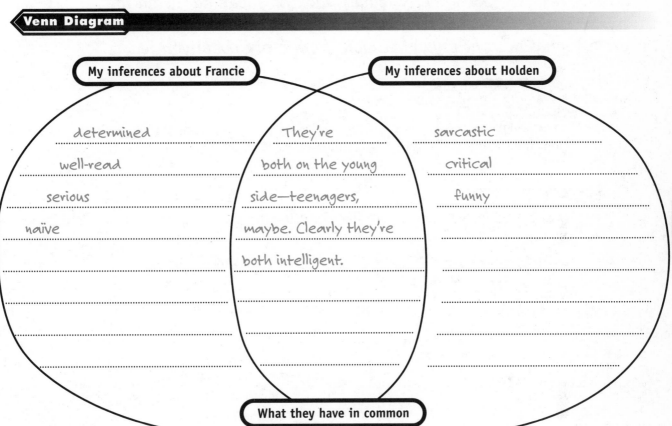

My inferences about Francie

My inferences about Holden

determined

well-read

serious

naïve

They're both on the young side—teenagers, maybe. Clearly they're both intelligent.

sarcastic

critical

funny

What they have in common

Fiction

Step 3 Draw conclusions.

As a final step, draw conclusions about the similarities and differences between the two works.

Directions: Complete these two sentences.

Francie and Holden are similar in that they are both young, and they are both clearly intelligent and perceptive.

They are different in these ways: Francie seems naïve, and Holden seems kind of bitter, like he's seen it all. I can't imagine Holden thinking that he could read every book in the library, and I can't imagine Francie being critical of her school.

Reading a Poem

Reading poetry takes time and patience but has great rewards. Good poetry readers look for meaning, listen for sounds, and try to visualize a poem's images. Use the reading process to help you get more from every poem you read.

Before Reading

Here you'll use the reading process and the strategy of close reading to help you understand and respond to a poem called "Sympathy."

 A **Set a Purpose**

Just as you do with any other type of writing, begin by setting your purpose.

- **To set your purpose, ask questions about the subject, mood, and meaning of the poem.**

<u>Directions:</u> Write your purpose questions for reading "Sympathy" below. Then, make a prediction about the poem.

My purpose questions: What is "Sympathy" about?

How does the poem make me feel?

What does the author want me to know?

My prediction: I predict that this poem will be about a death, like a loved one dying.

That's what I think of when I hear the word <u>sympathy.</u>

NAME ....

B Preview

Before you begin reading a poem, always spend a moment or two previewing it. This will help you get a sense of what the poem is about.

Directions: Preview "Sympathy." Then make some preview notes.

◄ Preview Chart

The title: "Sympathy"

The poet's name: Paul Laurence Dunbar

From the background information I learned that: The poet lived around 100 years ago. He worked first as an elevator operator and sold his poems to the passengers who rode his elevator.

The subject of the poem is: Something about a caged bird.

I saw these repeated words and phrases: I know why; caged bird; first

Here's what I noticed about the shape and structure of the poem: The poem has three stanzas, with seven lines in each stanza. Several lines end with a long dash.

I noticed this about the rhyme scheme: Every other line rhymes.

Poetry

Paul Laurence Dunbar (1872–1906) was the son of slaves who escaped by way of the Underground Railroad. From an early age, Paul showed talent for writing and dreamed of becoming a lawyer. Because there was no money to spare for college, however, Paul took a job as an elevator operator. When he was twenty-one years old, Paul published his first volume of poetry, which he sold to passengers who rode his elevator. Soon he had sold enough of his work that he was able to quit his job as an elevator operator and begin writing for a living. In many of his short stories and poems, Dunbar explored themes of slavery and pre-Civil War life in the South.

"Sympathy" by Paul Laurence Dunbar

I know what the caged bird feels, alas!
When the sun is bright on the upland slopes;
When the wind stirs soft through the springing grass,
And the river flows like a stream of glass;
When the first bird sings and the first bud opes,
And the faint perfume from its chalice steals — —
I know what the caged bird feels!

I know why the caged bird beats his wing
Till its blood is red on the cruel bars;
For he must fly back to his perch and cling
When he fain would be on the bough a-swing;
And a pain still throbs in the old, old scars
And they pulse again with a keener sting — —
I know why he beats his wing!

I know why the caged bird sings, ah me,
When his wing is bruised and his bosom sore — —
When he beats his bars and he would be free;
It is not a carol of joy or glee,
But a prayer that he sends from his heart's deep core,
But a plea, that upward to Heaven he flings — —
I know why the caged bird sings!

Who or what is the subject of this poem?
A caged bird

What is the rhyme scheme? ABAABCC.

What is the mood?
The mood seems a little sad, but a little angry too.

Why do you think the poet repeats the phrase "I know why the caged bird"? He wants the reader to know that he himself has experienced these things.

C Plan

After your preview, choose a strategy that can help you understand and respond to the poem.

• **Use the strategy of close reading with poetry.**

During Reading

D Read with a Purpose

Plan on reading a poem several times. This way you won't have to worry about understanding everything at once.

Directions: Read "Sympathy" several times. Make notes on the organizer below.

Plan for Reading a Poem

First and Second Readings	Third and Fourth Readings	Fifth Reading
Here's what I liked about the poem:	This is what I noticed about the structure:	This is my reaction to the poem:
I liked that it was easy to read. There are no hard words or lines that are hard to understand. Also, the punctuation is pretty normal.	The rhyme scheme is ABAABCC. The meter seems to be regular.	I really liked it. I especially like some of the phrases: "caged bird," stream of glass, carol of joy or glee, and so on.
This is what I think the poet is saying:	This is the mood of the poem:	
I think he is making a comparison between a caged bird and a human slave.	The mood is partly sad and partly angry. The speaker sounds angriest in the third stanza.	

Poetry

Using the Strategy

Remember that close reading means reading line for line, word for word.

- **Use a Double-entry Journal to keep track of your responses to words and lines in a poem.**

Directions: Read the quoted lines from Dunbar's poem. Then, write what the words mean or how they make you feel.

Double-entry Journal

Quote	My Thoughts and Feelings
I know what the caged bird feels, alas!	The "alas" tells me that the speaker has been a "caged bird" at one time or another.
Till its blood is red on the cruel bars;	This is from the second stanza. The speaker is becoming angrier. You can tell because his images are more violent.
But a plea, that upward to Heaven he flings	This is from the third stanza. It's strange to think of a prayer as something that you "fling." This shows the desperation of the "caged bird."

Understanding How Poems Are Organized

Good poets know that the organization or structure of a poem can contribute to its meaning. For example, a poet will use rhyme to create a certain effect or repetition to draw attention to a certain idea.

Directions: Go back and reread Dunbar's poem. Think about how it sounds and looks. Make notes on the stickies that are provided.

 E Connect

Making a personal connection to a poem will help you understand it. This in turn will enhance your enjoyment of the work.

- **Connect to a poem by recording your thoughts and feelings about both the sound and meaning of the work.**

NAME

Directions: Reflect on Dunbar's poem. Then complete the following sentences.

◄ Connection Comments

When I read the poem, I felt: confused at first, and couldn't figure out what the caged bird thing meant. But then I started to feel sort of sad. I felt the "sympathy" of the title.

I felt this because: the "caged bird" is a metaphor for people held as slaves. The poem is about how these people felt in captivity. They would try to free themselves, but it was futile a lot of the time.

How the speaker of the poem feels about slavery: He thinks it's horrible.

I know this because: In this poem, slaves are like birds in cages. No matter what they do or say or sing, they remain locked up.

After Reading

When you finish reading, take a moment or two to think about what you did and did not understand about a poem.

Pause and Reflect

Never leave a poem until you're sure you understand what all of it means.

> • **After you finish a poem, ask yourself, "Have I answered my purpose questions?"**

Directions: Circle one of the answers below. Then explain your answer.

I feel I (have)/ have not met my reading purpose. Here's why: I think I pretty much understand what the poet is saying. He's comparing a man or woman held as a slave to a caged bird.

Reread

Once you understand a poem, you can relax and enjoy it. "Listen" to the rhythm of the verse. Think about the message the poet has for you.

> • **A powerful rereading strategy to use with poetry is paraphrasing.**

Poetry

Directions: Reread Dunbar's poem one last time. Then, make notes in the Paraphrase Chart below.

Paraphrase Chart

Lines from the Poem	My Paraphrase
When the first bird sings and the first bud opes	This means that the speaker knows how the caged bird feels when all around him life is sweet, but he has no freedom to enjoy it.
I know why the caged bird beats his wing/ Till its blood is red on the cruel bars	This means that the speaker understands the bird's frustration. The bird knows escape is impossible, but still he bangs his wings against the bars of the cage.
It is not a carol of joy or glee,/ But a prayer that he sends from his heart's deep core	A caged bird's song is its plea for freedom. Slaves often sang as they worked. I think their songs were also prayers to heaven for freedom.

 Remember

When you finish reading, do a little writing. It will help you better remember what you've read.

• **Writing can help you remember a poem's subject and meaning.**

Directions: Write a letter in which you describe "Sympathy" and what it meant to you.

Letter

Hi,

Today in English class we read a poem called "Sympathy" by Paul Laurence Dunbar. In this poem, Dunbar compares a slave's life to a caged bird's life. He says that he knows how a caged bird feels and why he beats his wings against the bars of the cage and sings. He's saying that slaves did the same thing, wanting to win their freedom. But sometimes their efforts were as futile as those of a caged bird.

Focus on Language

*In most cases when reading a poem, it's the language—
the individual words and phrases—that captures your
attention first.*

Step 1 Read for key words.

On your first or second reading of a poem, watch for key words, especially
words that describe an action, create a mood, or name a person, place,
or thing.

Directions: Read "The Tyger." Underline words that grab your attention.
Then, make notes on the stickies.

"The Tyger" by William Blake

Tyger! Tyger! burning bright!
In the forests of the night,
What immortal hand or eye
Could frame thy fearful symmetry?

In what distant deeps or skies
Burnt the fire of thine eyes?
On what wings dare he aspire?
What the hand dare seize the fire?

And what shoulder, and what art,
Could twist the sinews of thy heart?
And when thy heart began to beat,
What dread hand and what dread feet?

What the hammer? what the chain?
In what furnace was thy brain?
What the anvil? what dread grasp
Dare its deadly terrors clasp?

When the stars threw down their spears,
And watered heaven with their tears,
Did He smile His work to see?
Did He who made the Lamb, make thee?

> what is the subject
> of the poem? a tiger or
> tigers

Poetry

"The Tyger" by William Blake

Tyger! Tyger! burning bright,
In the forests of the night,
What <u>immortal</u> hand or eye
Dare frame thy fearful <u>symmetry</u>?

How does the poet feel about the subject?

I think the poet admires the strength and beauty of the tiger but is afraid of him, too.

Step 2 Think about word connotations.

Connotation is the feeling conveyed by a word. The connotation of the words in a poem can also point toward its meaning.

Directions: Read the words in the left-hand column. Write their connotations on the right.

Word Connotations

Words from the Poem	Feelings They Convey
burning, immortal, fearful, seize, dread, anvil, deadly	These words all convey feelings of violence or fear. Through these words, the speaker is saying that a tiger is a deadly animal.

Step 3 Look for figurative language, imagery, and repetition.

Figurative language, imagery, and repetition give depth and meaning to a poem.

Directions: Look at the examples of imagery in "The Tyger" in the chart on the next page. Write down in the chart what you think the phrases mean and what sense or senses you use to experience the words. Then, make notes about repetition in the poem.

Imagery Chart

Imagery from the Poem	What I Think It Means	The Sense or Senses I Use
In the forests of the night	The tiger prowls in darkness.	sight
What the hand dare seize the fire?	This means that it would be as dangerous to touch a tiger as it would be to touch fire.	touch

These words are repeated in "The Tyger": tyger, burning bright, fire, dread, dare, forests, night

The repetition tells me that the poet understands the strength and fury of the tiger.

Poetry

Step 4 Consider the tone and mood.

As a final step, think about the tone and mood of the poem.

Directions: Record your thoughts about tone and mood in a journal entry.

Journal

The tone of this poem is respectful and admiring, as if the poet is in awe of the tiger. It's almost as if the speaker is saying, "Wow! I can't believe how incredible a tiger is." The mood the poet conveys is one of wonder, like he wants his readers to see, hear, and feel the magnificence of this animal.

Focus on Meaning

As you've seen, close reading is the best way to read and understand a poem. Follow these steps to get at the exact meaning.

Step 1 Examine the poem's language.

First, read the poem the whole way through without stopping. Then examine individual words.

Directions: Read this excerpt from a poem. Circle words that seem interesting or important. Then, make notes on the sticky.

from " 'For oh,' say the children, 'we are weary' " by Elizabeth Barrett Browning

"For oh," say the children, "we are weary
And we cannot run or leap;
If we cared for any meadows, it were merely
To drop down in them and sleep.
Our knees tremble sorely in the stooping,
We fall upon our faces, trying to go;
And underneath our heavy eyelids drooping
The reddest flower would look as pale as snow.
For, all day, we drag our burden tiring
Through the coal-dark underground;
Or, all day, we drive the wheels of iron
In the factories, round and round. . . ."

What would you say is the connotation of the words weary, stooping, drooping, and coal-dark? They all have negative connotations.

What is the effect of these words? They create a dark and unhappy sense when used all together.

Step 2 Think about the poet's style.

Style is how the author uses language. Some of the many stylistic elements are figurative language, imagery, rhythm, and word choice.

Directions: Think about the style of Browning's poem. Then, complete this Double-entry Journal.

◀ **Double-entry Journal** ▶

Browning's Words	My Thoughts
pale as snow	This is an example of a simile. It draws attention to how worn-out, cold, and sickly the children are.
coal-dark underground	This is imagery. The places the children work are as dark as night. Browning is also saying that children work in coal mines.
heavy eyelids drooping	The rhythm is slow and drawn out. This sounds like being almost asleep or being very, very tired.

Poetry

Step 3 Reflect on the poet's attitude.

This formula can help you find the message of a poem:

topic of the poem   +   what the poet is saying about the topic   =   the poet's message

Directions: Use the formula to find Browning's message in "'For oh,' say the children, 'We are weary.'"

Subject of the poem	+	What Browning says	=	The poet's message
child labor		It makes the children tired and		The practice of
		robs them of their health.		child labor is cruel
	+		**=**	and horrible.

Step 4 Listen to your own feelings.

Ask yourself, "How does the poem make me feel?"

Directions: Write your feelings about Browning's poem.

The poem makes me feel   sad and angry   because   the children who have to work in

these factories and mines are so exhausted and pathetic.

NAME ....

Focus on Sound and Structure

Sound and structure are yet more elements of a poem for you to understand. To focus on sound and structure, examine how the poem looks, and listen to how it sounds.

Step 1 Do a careful reading.

First, read the poem the whole way through without stopping. Then make some notes about how it looks and sounds.

Directions: Read this poem by Thomas Hardy. Make notes on the stickies.

"Throwing a Tree" by Thomas Hardy

The two executioners stalk along over the knolls,
Bearing two axes with heavy heads shining and wide,
And a long limp two-handled saw toothed for cutting great boles,
And so they approach the prod tree that bears the death-mark on its side.

Jackets doffed they swing axes and chop away just above the ground,
And the chips fly about and lie white on the moss and fallen leaves;
Till a broad deep gash in the bark is hewn all the way round,
And one of them tries to hook upward a rope, which at last he achieves.

The saw then begins, till the top of the tall giant shivers:
The shivers are seen to grow greater each cut than before:
They edge out the saw, tug the rope; but the tree only quivers,
And kneeling and sawing again, they step back to try pulling once more.

Then, lastly, the living mast sways, further sways: with a shout
Job and Ike rush aside. Reached the end of its long staying powers
The tree crashes downward: it shakes all its neighbours throughout,
And two hundred years' steady growth has been ended in less than two hours.

How many stanzas does the poem have? 4

How many lines are there per stanza? 4

What do you notice about the rhyme? Every other line rhymes.

What do you notice about the final line of each stanza? It is set farther to the left.

Which repeated words grabbed your attention? axe, saw, shivers, tree, sways

Poetry

Step 2 Examine the organization.

The organization of a poem can offer clues about its meaning.

Directions: Reread "Throwing a Tree," and then summarize each stanza of Hardy's poem. Write your notes on this chart.

Stanza-by-Stanza Summary

Stanza	My Summary
1	Two men walk in the woods toward a particular tree. They carry axes and saws.
2	The men begin chopping away at the tree. One of the men throws a rope over the branches so that they can yank the tree down when they've made a deep enough cut.
3	The tree begins to fall. The men pull on the rope. The tree trembles and sways.
4	The two men jump out of the way, and the tree falls. The speaker ends by saying that it took just a few hours for a tree that is two hundred years old to fall.

Step 3 Listen for repeated sounds.

Next, listen to the "music" of the poem. What do the words sound like? What do they remind you of? What effect do they create?

Directions: Look for examples of repetition, alliteration, and assonance in "Throwing a Tree." If you need help with these terms, see pages 418–419 in the *Reader's Handbook*.

Poetic Sounds Chart

Repeated words: axe, shivers, saw, tree, sways, they

Stanza	Alliteration (repeated consonant sounds)	Assonance (repeated vowel sounds)
1	two, toothed, tree; stalk, saw, side	o sound: stalk, along, boles
2	chop, chips, fly, fallen	a sound: axes, a, all, achieves
3	till, top, tall, tug, tree, try; saw, shivers, seen, sawing	i sound: till, shivers, quivers
4	sways, shout, staying, shakes, steady; lastly, living, long, less	a sound: lastly, mast, aside, all, has

NAME ....

Step 4 Explore the rhyme and rhythm.

Poets use rhyme and rhythm for many reasons, including:

- to establish a mood
- to bring emphasis to an idea
- to keep the reader interested and enhance his or her enjoyment

Directions: Answer the following questions about the rhyme and rhythm in "Throwing a Tree."

Rhyme and Rhythm Questions

1. What is the rhyme scheme in Hardy's poem? The rhyme scheme is abab, cdcd, and so on.

2. Does it change from stanza to stanza? Yes, each stanza has different end rhymes, but the basic pattern remains the same.

3. What is the meter of the poem? There are seven beats per line, except for the last line of each stanza.

4. At what point does the meter change? What is the effect of this change? It changes at the final line of each stanza. This puts additional emphasis on the terrible action of the men.

Step 5 Put it all together.

As a final step, use your notes about sound and structure to help you make inferences about the meaning of the poem.

Directions: Use this Double-entry Journal to organize your thoughts about the meaning of Hardy's poem.

Double-entry Journal

What I Know about the Sound and Structure	My Thoughts and Ideas
The poem tells a story. It relates a series of events that end in the felling of a tree. The regular rhyme and rhythm keep you moving along from one line to another and also draw your attention to the final line of each stanza. There are lots of repeated words and sounds. I notice that many of them are violent words like stalk, saw, shivers, and shakes.	By focusing on the sound and structure, I was able to see that the speaker of the poem is definitely not happy that the two men have chopped down the tree. He seems angry about it, and that's why he chooses so many "angry" words.

Poetry

Reading a Play

A play is different from a story in that the action in a play is told entirely through the dialogue and stage directions. Your job as a reader is to listen carefully to what each character says and visualize what the characters are doing and describing.

Before Reading

Use the reading process and the strategy of summarizing to get more from every play you read. Practice here with an excerpt from *Oedipus the King* by Sophocles.

 A ## Set a Purpose

Your purpose will be the same no matter what play you are reading.

- **To set your purpose, ask questions about the setting, characters, conflict, and theme of the play.**

Directions: Write your purpose for reading *Oedipus the King* below. Then write what you already know about this play.

Purpose Questions:

Where and when does this play take place?

Who is Oedipus, and what was he like?

What happens between the characters in the play?

What is the chief conflict?

What are the themes?

What I know about the play:

   I know that Sophocles lived a long, long time ago, like in ancient times before Shakespeare. I've

heard of Oedipus from the phrase an <u>Oedipal Complex</u>, but I don't know what he did or why

Sophocles wanted to write a play about him.

B Preview

Be sure to preview a play before you begin reading. Look for both setting and character clues. Try to get a sense of what the play is about.

Directions: Preview the title page for *Oedipus the King*. Make notes on the stickies.

> from *Oedipus the King* by Sophocles

ARGUMENT

To Laius, King of Thebes, an oracle foretold that the child born to him by his queen Jocasta would slay his father and wed his mother. So when in time a son was born the infant's feet were tied together and he was left to die on Mount Cithaeron. But a shepherd found the babe and saved him, and delivered him to another shepherd who took him to his master, the King of Corinth. Polybus being childless adopted the boy, who grew up believing that he was indeed the king's son. Afterwards doubting his parentage he inquired of the Delphic god and heard himself the weird oracle foretold before to Laius. So Oedipus fled from what he deemed his father's house and in his flight he encountered and unwillingly slew his father Laius. Arriving at Thebes he answered the riddle of the Sphinx and the grateful Thebans made their deliverer king. So he reigned in the room of Laius and married Jocasta, the widowed queen. Children were born to them and Thebes prospered under his rule, but again a grievous plague fell upon the city. Again the oracle was consulted and it bade them purge themselves of blood-guiltiness. Oedipus denounces the crime of which he is unaware, and undertakes to track out the criminal. Step by step it is brought home to him that he is the man. The closing scene reveals Jocasta slain by her own hand and Oedipus blinded by his own act and praying for death or exile.

DRAMATIS PERSONAE
Oedipus.
The Priest of Zeus.
Creon.
Chorus of Theban Elders.
Teiresias.
Jocasta.
Messenger.
Herd of Laius.
Second Messenger.

SETTING
Time: 430 B.C.
Place: Thebes

Sticky note (bottom left):
The setting is
Thebes in 430 B.C.
There are 9
characters.

Sticky note (right):
This is what I learned from the "Argument": According to the Delphic oracle, King Laius would be killed by his son, who would then marry his mother. To prevent this from happening, Laius leaves his son Oedipus to die. But he is saved and grows up to unknowingly kill his father and marry his mother. Then Oedipus must pay for his crime.

Drama

from *Oedipus the King* by Sophocles

SCENE 2: *Thebes. Before the palace of Oedipus.*
[Enter TEIRESIAS, led by a boy.]

OEDIPUS. Teiresias, seer who understands all of heaven and earth, although thou
    blinded eyes see nothing. A plague infects our city; and we turn to thee, O seer, as
    our only hope. The messengers have no doubt told thee—how we have but one
    choice, and that is to find Laius's murderers and deal with them. Then and only
    then will we find relief from our suffering. Therefore, tell us all, and keep nothing
    from us, so that you may save thyself, thy country, and thy king, and all that is
    touched by this deadly disease. We put our hopes on you, Teiresias. This is man's
    highest end, to others' service all his powers to lend.

TEIRESIAS. Alas, alas, what misery it is to be wise, when wisdom can do no good!
    But how horrible this old story is, and how long I have forgotten it. I should not
    have come.

OEDIPUS. But why? What ails thee? Why this melancholy mood?

TEIRESIAS. Let me go home—prevent me not.

OEDIPUS. For shame! No true-born Theban patriot would refuse to answer!

TEIRESIAS. I see danger in thy words, O king, and I shall not add to it.

OEDIPUS. Oh speak, and withhold nothing, I beg you; if you can answer, then you

Stop and Organize

What is Oedipus saying here? Make notes on the Character Map on page 170.

TEIRESIAS. But you are blind! No! I shall not reveal my secrets, and nor will I
    reveal yours!

OEDIPUS. What then? You know and yet will not speak? Is it possible that you
    would betray us and the city in such a way?

TEIRESIAS. I will not cause you further grief, and I will not grieve myself. Why do
    you ask me such questions when you have no desire to learn?

OEDIPUS. Monster! Your silence would anger a rock. Will nothing loosen your
    tongue? Can nothing move you, or shake loose the truth from your lips?

TEIRESIAS. You blame my mood, and see not yourself. Know yourself, Oedipus. You
    denounce me, but you know nothing of yourself.

OEDIPUS. You expect me to control my rage after you have disgraced your city?
    How do you dare?

TEIRESIAS. But it does not matter if I speak. The future will come—it has already

NAME ....

from *Oedipus the King* by Sophocles

been set and cannot be changed.

OEDIPUS. Since come it must, your duty is to tell me.

Stop and Organize

How does Teiresias feel about Oedipus? Make notes on the Character Map on page 170.

OEDIPUS. Yes, I am enraged, and I will not be careful with my words—I will speak my whole mind and tell you what I think. I think this horrible crime was *your* doing. You did everything except commit the murder itself, and you would have done *that* had you not been blind! It is you who has done this bloody deed!

TEIRESIAS. Is that the truth? Then I ask you to listen to your own proclamation. From this day forward, deny yourself the right to speak to me or anyone. For it is you, Oedipus. You are the polluter of this land.

OEDIPUS. Vile slanderer! How dare you blame me? Do you think that you can tell these lies and then go free?

TEIRESIAS. Yea, I am free. I remain strong, with truth as my protector.

OEDIPUS. But who told you this? It came from no prophecy—I know that to be true.

TEIRESIAS. It is *you* who taught me. You forced me to say this, against my will.

OEDIPUS. Then say your speech again. I want no doubt in my mind.

TEIRESIAS. Are you trying to provoke me to more anger? Is that your aim?

OEDIPUS. No. I only half caught your meaning. I want to hear it all again so that I am sure.

TEIRESIAS. I say *you* are the murderer of Laius. You are the murderer that you have been searching for!

OEDIPUS. But again! You have said this again, and in repeating it have made yet a larger mistake.

TEIRESIAS. Shall I tell you more? You are angry enough to hear.

OEDIPUS. Say what you will. It will all be a waste of breath.

TEIRESIAS. I say you live in shame with your nearest kin. Without knowing it, you commit the ugliest of sins.

OEDIPUS. Do you think I will allow you to speak like this forever?

TEIRESIAS. If the truth is to prevail, then I shall be permitted to speak.

OEDIPUS. Other men speak the truth. But you—you are a fool. You are blind, you

Stop and Organize

How does Oedipus act in this scene? Make notes on the Character Map on page 170.

Drama

> ### from *Oedipus the King* by Sophocles
>
> TEIRESIAS. You're a fool to insult me for telling the truth. One day you will know that
> I've told no lies.
> OEDIPUS. You are a man of the endless night, Teiresias. And so you cannot hurt me,
> just as you cannot hurt any man who sees the light.
> TEIRESIAS. True, it is not I that will cause your downfall. I leave that to the god Apollo.
> OEDIPUS. Was this a trick from Creon—or was it your own?
> TEIRESIAS. No, not Creon, and not my own. You destroy your own self, Oedipus.

C Plan

After your preview, make a plan. Choose a strategy that can help you
understand the characters, actions, and themes of the play.

- **Use the strategy of summarizing to help you keep track of important
elements in a play.**

During Reading

D Read with a Purpose

There are several different tools that you can use with the strategy of
summarizing. One that works particularly well is a Character Map.

Directions: Do a careful reading of the argument and scene 2 from *Oedipus
the King*. Make notes about Oedipus on the Character Map.

Character Map

What the character says and does	What others think about the character
He is talking to Teiresias about the horrible "plague" on the city that comes as a result of the murder of King Laius. He demands that Teiresias give him some answers.	Teiresias is pretty patient with Oedipus at first, and then he gets really mad. He is disgusted that Oedipus tries to bully him this way.

Oedipus

How the character acts and feels	How I feel about the character
Oedipus is frustrated and angry. He wants to solve the murder and lift the plague from his city. But he is also too proud to believe that he could be the cause of all these problems.	He seems sort of pig-headed. He's the type who won't listen to anyone and then gets in trouble for it.

Using the Strategy

Use a Magnet Summary to explore the big ideas you find in a play. These big ideas may point the way to important themes.

Directions: An important idea in Oedipus is "blindness." Skim the excerpt to see how many mentions of being blind or blindness you find. Then, complete this Magnet Summary.

Magnet Summary

blind in the physical sense:

Teiresias

blind to the truth: Oedipus

Oedipus is blind to the fact that he has killed his father and married his mother.

blindness

Oedipus assumes that because Teiresias is blind, he cannot see the truth.

Although Teiresias is blind, he can "see" all that goes on in heaven and on earth.

The word blindness has many meaning's in this play. Teiresias is "blind," but he sees the truth,

Oedipus is "blind" to what he has done when he kills his father and marries his mother.

Drama

Understanding How Plays Are Organized

Plays are divided into acts and scenes. Each act or scene moves the characters closer to the climax of the plot.

- **Make a scene-by-scene summary to keep track of what happens in a play. Reread what you've written if you find yourself lost.**

Directions: Read the summary for Scene 1 of *Oedipus the King*. Then write a summary for Scene 2.

Scene-by-Scene Summary

Part of Play	Setting	Key Events
Scene 1	outside the palace at Thebes	The citizens of Thebes beg Oedipus to rid the city of the plague. Oedipus explains that he sent his brother-in-law, Creon, to the oracle at Delphi to get help. Creon returns and tells Oedipus that the only way to stop the plague is for Oedipus to find and banish the murderer of King Laius.
Scene 2	outside the palace at Thebes	Oedipus begs Teiresias the prophet to reveal the murderer of Laius. Teiresias refuses, and they argue. Finally, he gets mad at Oedipus and tells him that it is he who killed Laius. Oedipus refuses to believe Teiresias and calls him a fool.

Connect

Making a personal connection to a play can help you think more critically about what you've read.

• **Connect to a play by recording your thoughts and feelings about the characters and action.**

<u>Directions:</u> Reread this short speech from *Oedipus the King*. Then write your reaction.

> OEDIPUS. Yes, I am enraged, and I will not be careful with my words—I will speak my whole mind and tell you what I think. I think this horrible crime was *your* doing. You did everything except commit the murder itself, and you would have done *that* had you not been blind! It is you who has done this bloody deed!

I think Oedipus is a fool because he blames everyone but himself. He doesn't want to see the truth.

 After Reading

When you finish a play, think about what you've learned.

 Pause and Reflect

Ask yourself about the characters, setting, conflict, and theme.

• **Always check to see if you've met your original reading purpose.**

<u>Directions:</u> How well did you meet your reading purpose? What would you like to find out more about? Explain here.

I'd like to read more of this play. I'm kind of curious to see what happens to Oedipus. My big question is whether it is really true that Oedipus killed Laius, and if so, why did he do it? I'd also like to find out about that business with Oedipus's wife. Is she really Oedipus's mother? How did that happen?

Drama

Reread

An important part of reading a play is visualizing the action. This can be very helpful if you are having a hard time understanding what happens in a particular scene.

• **A powerful rereading strategy to use is visualizing and thinking aloud. It can help you "see" important ideas in the play.**

Directions: Draw a picture of Oedipus and Teiresias in front of the palace of Thebes. Then, write a caption that summarizes what is happening.

 Sketch

Oepidus argues with Teiresias in front of the palace.

 Remember

It is important to find a way to remember what you've read.

• **Performing an oral reading of a key scene can help you recall important elements of the play.**

Directions: Choose a short passage from *Oedipus the King*. Write the passage here. Then, get together with a partner and discuss why you chose this particular passage.

Passage from Oedipus the King:

TEIRESIAS. You're a fool to insult me for telling the truth. One day you will know that I've told no lies.

OEDIPUS. You are a man of the endless night, Teiresias. And so you cannot hurt me, just as you

cannot hurt any man who sees the light.

TEIRESIAS. True, it is not I that will cause your downfall. I leave that to the god Apollo.

OEDIPUS. Was this a trick from Creon—or was it your own?

TEIRESIAS. No, not Creon, and not my own. You destroy your own self, Oedipus.

Why I chose this passage: I love the fact that Teiresias is hammering home the truth here,

and that Oedipus is going to have to accept what he has said.

Focus on Language

Focusing on dramatic language means analyzing the key lines and speeches, stage directions, and the dialogue between characters in a play. Follow these steps.

Step 1 Examine key lines and speeches.

When you read a play, always keep an eye out for the key lines and speeches. They will give you important clues about a character's personality.

Directions: Read this speech from *Oedipus the King*. Then, write adjectives that describe Teiresias on the sticky.

from *Oedipus the King* by Sophocles

TEIRESIAS. I will go when I've said all that I came to say. I am not afraid of you. You cannot hurt me. And I tell you this: The man you seek—the man whose death or banishment you ordered, the man who murdered Laius—that man is here, living in our midst. Soon it will be known to all of you—he is a native Thebian. And he will find no joy in that discovery. His eyes now see, but soon they will be blind; rich now, but soon a beggar. . . .

> Adjectives that describe
>
> Teiresias: truthful, determined,
>
> head-strong—he'll say what he has
>
> come to say, no matter what.

Step 2 Read the stage directions.

Reading the stage directions makes it easier for you to visualize the action of a play. They can give you clues about setting and action.

Drama

Directions: Read these stage directions from Scene 1 of *Oedipus the King*. Make notes on the stickies.

Scene: *In front of the doors at the palace of Oedipus at Thebes. A crowd of citizens sits at an altar in supplication. Among them is an old man, the priest of Zeus.*

Where does the opening scene take place? In Thebes, at the palace of Oedipus

Who is there? A crowd of Thebians along with the priest of Zeus

Step 3 Analyze the dialogue.

Dialogue can point the way to a play's theme.

Directions: Read this conversation between Oedipus and a shepherd who knows the truth about the king. Look for a line that supports Sophocles' theme of blindness. Write the line in the organizer and then explain what it means.

from *Oedipus the King* by Sophocles

OEDIPUS. But this prophecy! What was it, good Shephard?

SHEPHERD. The prophecy said that the child would kill his father.

OEDIPUS. Then why did you give the baby away? Why did you not kill it?

SHEPHERD. I felt sorry for him, master. And I thought that he would take the babe to his own home. But he saved the babe from his suffering—for worse suffering yet. My Lord, if you are the man he says you are—O god—you were born for suffering!

OEDIPUS. O God! O no! I see it now! All clear! O Light! I will never look on you again! Sin! Sin in my birth! Sin in my marriage! Sin in blood!

Double-entry Journal

Quote	My Thoughts
O God! O no! I see it now!	At last, Oedipus "sees" the truth about himself. He understands he has killed his father and married his mother.

Focus on Theme

The theme of a play is the writer's message. Use this three-step plan to find and evaluate a playwright's theme.

Step 1 Look for repeated words and symbols.

First, look for repeated words and symbols in a play. Some of these will point to the general topics the playwright is exploring.

Directions: Think about the key words and symbols in *Oedipus the King*. Write them on the Web below.

◄ **Web**

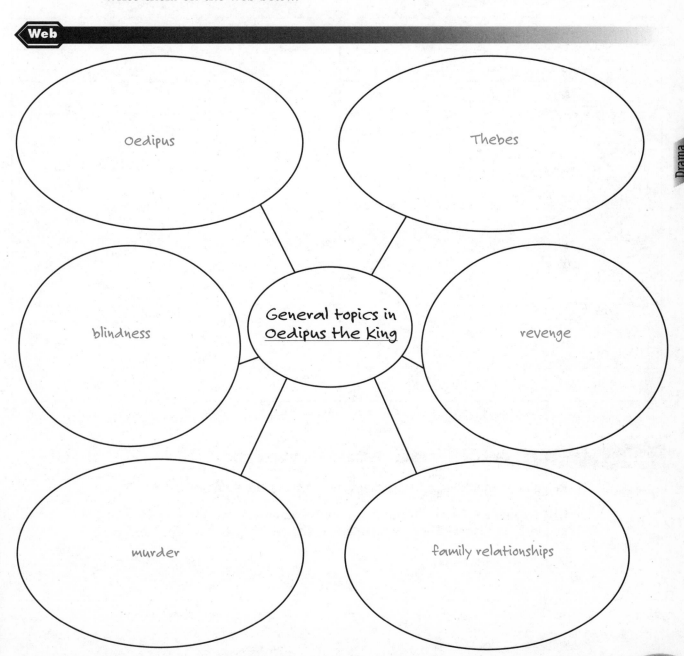

Oedipus

Thebes

blindness

General topics in <u>Oedipus the King</u>

revenge

murder

family relationships

Drama

Step 2 Note what the characters say and do.

Next, think about what the characters say and do that relate to these general topics.

Directions: Choose one general topic from your Web to explore. Write what Oedipus and Teiresias say about the topic.

General Topic: blindness

What Oedipus Says	What Teiresias Says
calls Teiresias a "seer"	says "I see danger in thy words, O king."
says Teiresias is blind and his mind is crippled.	calls Oedipus "blind" to the truth about the murder

---

Step 3 Write a theme statement.

Remember that theme is the playwright's message about the topic.

Directions: Read the information about finding a theme on page 483 in the *Reader's Handbook*. Then, complete the Theme Organizer on the next page.

NAME ....

Theme Organizer

Topic: Blindness

Detail #1:

Oedipus says Teiresias is
blind and his mind is crippled.

Detail #2:

"I see danger in thy words, O
king."

Detail #3:

Teiresias calls Oedipus
"blind" to the truth about
the murder.

Theme:

You can see perfectly well and still be blind, just as
you can be blind and see perfectly well.

Drama

Focus on Shakespeare

The reading process and the strategy of using graphic organizers can help you read, understand, and respond to the plays by William Shakespeare.

Step 1 Read for sense.

First, read a passage once or twice. Use context clues and the footnotes to help you with difficult words.

Directions: Read this passage from *A Midsummer Night's Dream*. In this scene, a young man named Lysander speaks to Hermia, the woman he loves.

from *A Midsummer Night's Dream* by William Shakespeare

LYSANDER: . . . hear me, Hermia.
I have a widow aunt, a dowager
Of great revenue, and she hath no child.
From Athens is her house remote seven leagues;
And she respects me as her only son.   5
There, gentle Hermia, may I marry thee,
And to that place the sharp Athenian law
Cannot pursue us. If thou lovest me, then,
Steal forth thy father's house tomorrow night;
And in the wood, a league without the town,   10
Where I did meet thee once with Helena
To do observance to a morn of May,
There will I stay for thee.

5 **respects** regards
11 **without** outside

This is what Lysander is saying to Hermia: He is suggesting that they elope and sets up the spot for a rendezvous.

NAME ....

Step 2 Read for specifics.

When you read for specifics, you read to understand the important literary elements of the work. Using graphic organizers can help.

Directions: Read the text in the left-hand column. Write what it tells you about Lysander on the right.

◄ Inference Chart ▶

Text	What It Tells Me About the Character
There, gentle Hermia, may I marry thee,	Lysander is in love with a woman named Hermia.
Steal forth thy father's house tomorrow night;	Hermia's father does not approve of Lysander as a suitor for his daughter.

Step 3 Reflect.

Reacting or making personal connections to a Shakespearean play can heighten your enjoyment of the work. It can also help you think critically about the action, characters, or scene.

Directions: Reflect on the experiences you have had reading Shakespeare. Then, explain what you enjoy about his work and what makes it challenging for you.

When I read Shakespeare, I enjoy the beautiful sentiments of the language. It is all so dramatic and fun. I also love all the characters he created and invented.

This is what I find challenging Much as I love the language, it is often very hard to figure out what Shakespeare is saying. I have to work very hard when I am reading the plays.

Drama

Reading a Website

Always read a website with a critical eye. Zero in on the information you need, and then double-check to see if it's reliable.

Before Reading

Practice using the reading process and the strategy of reading critically with a website designed for sports fans.

A Set a Purpose

It's easy to lose your way on the Internet. One false click, and you're lost in a jungle of unfamiliar websites. To prevent this from happening, set your purpose *before* accessing a website.

• **To set your purpose, make a list of questions about the subject.**

__Directions:__ Use this K-W-L Chart to record your areas of expertise when it comes to sports. Then, write what you want to find out.

K-W-L Chart

What I Know	What I Want to Know	What I Learned
I know a lot about baseball, tennis, and basketball. I'm pretty familiar with the most famous players.	I need to know about other sports, like football, wrestling, and hockey. I'd like to find out which sports are the most popular and why.	I can use this website to find out about all professional and semi-professional teams. The site is affiliated with a university, so I think it's pretty reliable.

B Preview

It's vitally important that you preview a website before you begin clicking. This will give you a sense of what's offered and whether or not the site can help you meet your purpose.

Directions: Preview the sports fan website that follows. Check each item on this checklist. Make notes about what you find.

Preview Checklist

Preview Checklist	My Notes
☑ The name and overall look of the site	"sportsfans.com"
☑ The main menu or table of contents	lists various sports leagues and types of sports
☑ The source or sponsor	National Sports Clearinghouse, an affiliate of Bear Creek University
☑ Any descriptions of the site	tells "what's new, what's hot, and what's coming up in the world of sports"
☑ Any images or graphics that create a feeling	There are pictures of a basketball, boxing gloves, a football, a baseball glove, and a soccer ball, which gives a good idea of the range of sports covered by the site.
☑ The purpose of the site	to keep viewers informed about sports news

Internet

http://www.sportsfans.com/home.asp*

The National Sports
Association presents

SportsFans.com

Subscribers log in here

Click here for

MLB

NFL

NHL

NBA

NCAA Football

NCAA Basketball

PGA/WPGA

NASCAR

World Cup Tennis

Wrestling

Additional sports

SportsFans.com has been entertaining sports fans since 1993. This is your site for what's new, what's hot, and what's coming up in the world of sports. Here you can read about your favorite teams, your favorite leagues, and your favorite players. Our mission is to present equal and fair coverage of every team playing today in the professional and semi-professional leagues.

Fans are talking about . . .

The Final Four

Baseball's Season Openers

Looking Ahead to the Indy 500

click here for more on these subjects

SportsFans.com is a project of the National Sports Clearinghouse, an affiliate of Bear Creek University in Bear Creek, New York. Coach Jamelle Walber is director of this site. Direct your comments to Coach Walber at www.jwalber@sfs.com/.

This site is updated daily.
Last updated: August 23, 2003

*URL is not real.

NAME ....

FOR USE WITH PAGES 513–527

 Plan

Next, make a reading plan. Choose a strategy that can help you read and evaluate the information offered on the site. The strategy of reading critically may be your best choice.

- **Reading critically means asking yourself, "How much can I trust this website?"**

During Reading

 Read with a Purpose

Keep in mind your purpose questions as you examine the site. Remember that you want to find reliable information about the given topic. Use a Website Profiler to organize your notes.

Directions: Read the sportsfans.com website carefully. Make notes on the following Website Profiler.

◄ Website Profiler

URL http://www.sportsfans.com	
Sponsor National Sports Clearinghouse	**Date** Last updated February 23, 2002
Point of View Designed with the sports fan in mind. There are links to the various league web pages, in addition to news about current sports topics.	**Expertise** The site is affiliated with a university and is supervised by a coach, so I think the information should be fairly reliable.
Reaction/Evaluation I think this website looks pretty thorough. I'd be curious to see if I could find stats and scores for every game played on a given day.	

Using the Strategy

Before you can evaluate the information on a website, you also need to note the links it has to offer and if they are up-to-date. Use Study Cards to keep track of worthwhile links.

- **When you read critically, you keep track of which links can help you meet your purpose.**

Directions: Make notes about the sportsfans.com website on these Study Cards. Tell which links you should follow and explain why.

Internet

Study Cards

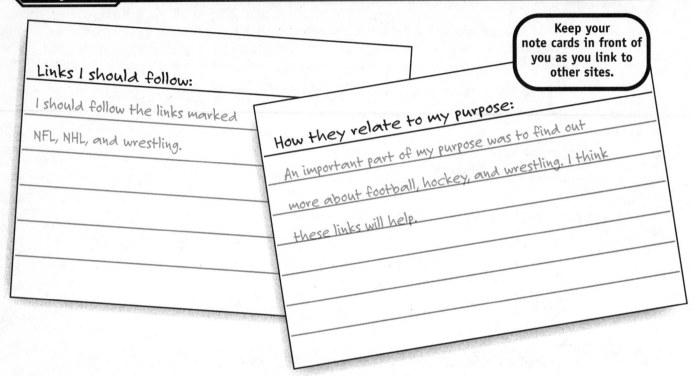

Links I should follow:

I should follow the links marked

NFL, NHL, and wrestling.

How they relate to my purpose:

An important part of my purpose was to find out

more about football, hockey, and wrestling. I think

these links will help.

Keep your note cards in front of you as you link to other sites.

Understanding How Websites Are Organized

A website looks like what it is called: a Web.

- **Map a website by creating a Web showing the links from the home page.**

Directions: Complete this Web. List three important links on the website. Predict what you think you'll find there.

Web

www.sportsfans.com

Link to NHL

stats, players, scores

Link to NFL

stats, standings, players

Link to Wrestling

matches, standings

Write what you'd expect to find at the links here.

E Connect

To get everything you can out of a website, think about how its ideas and content apply to you. An important part of this is deciding whether or not you want to return to the site again in the future.

- **Be sure to consider whether the website was of use to you personally.**

__Directions:__ Think of two websites you've visited recently. Explain your opinion of each site and why you will or will not return.

Connecting to a Website

Website #1 www.google.com

My opinion of it: It was pretty helpful. I needed to search for information about an artist and this search site gave me lots of "hits."

Why I will or will not return:

I'm sure I'll use the site again soon. It's simple to use, and it seems well organized.

Website #2 www.historyforkids.com

My opinion of it: It was pretty babyish. I can see my younger sister liking it, but this site is not for me.

Why I will or will not return:

I'm not going to bookmark this site. Instead, I'll search for a more academic history site.

After Reading

When you finish reading, take a moment or two to think about what you did and did not understand about the website. If the site has been helpful, make sure your notes are in good order before moving the mouse.

F Pause and Reflect

First, recall your original purpose for visiting the site.

- **As you finish using a website, ask yourself, "How well did I meet my purpose? Is there anything else I need to learn?"**

__Directions:__ Return to the K-W-L Chart on page 182 and complete the "L" column. Then, make some additional notes about the sportsfans.com site here.

I need to find out more about: specific statistics for football, hockey, and wrestling. I'd also like to learn a little about the history of these sports.

G Reread

There will be times that you'll want to return to a website to check a fact or search for additional information. Other times, you may want to evaluate the site as a whole. In both cases, the strategy of skimming can help.

• **Use the rereading strategy of skimming when checking the reliability of the information posted on a website.**

<u>Directions:</u> Read these questions. Skim the sportsfans.com website for answers.

Evaluating Internet Sources

1. Was the site updated recently? How often is it updated?	2. What is the source of the site?	3. What credentials does the site offer?	4. Are there any obvious errors on the site?
Yes. It is updated daily.	The National Sports Clearinghouse	It's affiliated with Bear Creek University.	None

These are the questions you should ask yourself when evaluating a website.

H Remember

Recording information on a graphic organizer can help you remember information from a website.

• **Use a graphic organizer to help you remember key elements of a website.**

<u>Directions:</u> Complete this graphic organizer about the sportsfans.com website.

Source Evaluator

Research Purpose	to find information about football, hockey, and wrestling
Title or Location	http://www.sportsfans.com
Date	February 23, 2002
Expertise	It seems reliable. It is affiliated with a university and is supervised by a coach.
Bias, if any	I don't see any signs of bias. They're not trying to sell me anything or convince me that something is true or accurate.
Reactions	I liked this site as it had a full set of links to information from the individual sports leagues.

NAME ....

Reading a Graphic

Graphics are visual representations of information. Your job when reading a graphic is to understand the information presented and then figure out why it is important. The reading process can help.

Before Reading

Use the reading process and the strategy of summarizing to help you read and respond to a graphic about electricity usage.

 ### A Set a Purpose

Most graphics contain words as well as visuals. Set a purpose that can help explore all of the elements of the graphic.

• **To set your purpose, ask two or more questions about the graphic.**

Directions: Write your purpose for reading a line graph that shows the number of kilowatt hours used each year from 1989 to 2001. Then make a prediction.

Purpose question #1: *What is the graphic about?*

....

....

Purpose question #2: *What does it show me? What conclusions can I draw?*

....

....

My prediction: *I predict the graphic will show that kilowatt-hour usage has increased each*

year since 1989.

....

Internet

B Preview

When you preview, ask yourself, "What is the big picture shown in this graphic?" Try to get a sense of what information is being offered, how it is organized, and why it might be important.

Directions: Preview the line graph shown below. Then, make some preview notes.

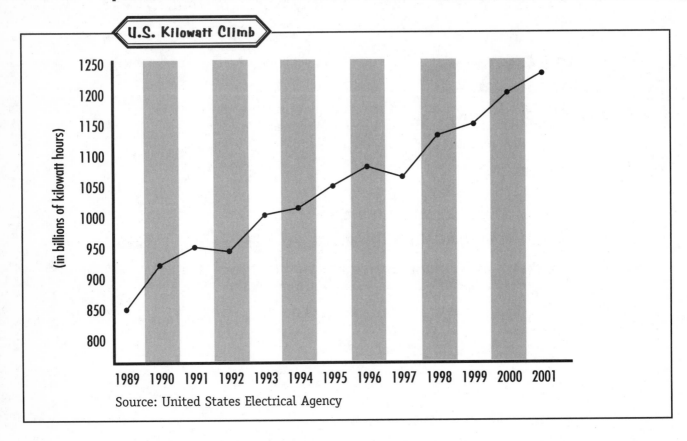

U.S. Kilowatt Climb

(in billions of kilowatt hours)

Source: United States Electrical Agency

Title of the graphic: "U.S. Kilowatt Climb"

Type of graphic: line graph

Dates represented: 1989–2001

Labels, column and row headings: I see years from 1989 to 2001. I also see that the numbers running up the left side of the graphic represent billions of kilowatt hours.

What is the big picture? The graphic shows that the number of kilowatt hours used by Americans has climbed drastically since 1989.

NAME ....

C Plan

Your next step is to make a plan. Choose a strategy that will help you read, interpret, and respond to the graphic.

• **The strategy of paraphrasing works well with most graphics because it can help you process the key facts and details.**

During Reading

Remember that in a graphic, the visual element and the text are equally important.

D Read with a Purpose

Reread the plan for reading a graphic on page 544 of the *Reader's Handbook*. Use this plan to interpret the kilowatt-hour line graph.

Directions: Read the kilowatt-hour line graph. Then paraphrase, or tell in your own words, what the graphic shows. Write your paraphrase on the lines below.

What the graphic shows: It shows that kilowatt-hour usage by Americans has increased

drastically since 1989. In 1989, Americans used 850 billion kilowatt hours. In 2001, Americans

used 1,225 billion kilowatt hours.

....

....

....

....

Graphics

Using the Strategy

When you paraphrase, you take key details from a text and put them in your own words. Using your own words can help you process and remember what you've read. A Paraphrase Chart can help.

Directions: Complete this Paraphrase Chart using information from the kilowatt graphic. See page 545 of the *Reader's Handbook* if you're not sure how to use this tool.

Paraphrase Chart

Title	"Kilowatt Climb"
My Paraphrase	The number of kilowatt hours used by Americans has increased dramatically since 1989. Although a couple of years showed a small decrease in hours used, overall usage has increased.
My Thoughts	My guess is that one reason there has been this huge increase in the amount of electricity used by Americans is because there has been a huge increase in the number of households that have one or more personal computers. I'd be interested in knowing what percentage of families had a personal computer in 1989 versus what percentage of families had one in 2001.

NAME

Understanding How Graphics Are Organized

Familiarize yourself with the key elements used in graphics. This will make it easier for you to read all the different types of graphics.

Directions: Label the following elements on the graphic below: *title, source, horizontal (x) axis,* and *vertical (y) axis.*

U.S. Kilowatt Climb — title

y axis

(in billions of kilowatt hours)

1989 1990 1991 1992 1993 1994 1995 1996 1997 1998 1999 2000 2001 — x axis

Source: United States Electrical Agency — source

1. How many kilowatt hours were used by Americans in 1989? 850 billion

2. How many additional kilowatt hours were used in 1990? 75 billion

3. What do you notice about the years 1992 and 1997? There were small drops in kilowatt usage from the previous years.

4. What would you predict would be the total kilowatt usage in 2002 using this graphic as evidence?

I predict the amount of kilowatt usage would continue to climb, by perhaps 50 or 75 billion kilowatt hours. That seems to be the general trend the previous ten or so years.

Graphics

E Connect

Understanding why the information in a graphic is important—and what it means to you personally—is an important part of reading critically.

• To connect to a graphic, ask yourself, "What does the information mean to me?"

Directions: Record your thoughts about the electricity graphic on this Double-entry Journal.

◄ Double-Entry Journal

What I Learned	My Thoughts and Reactions
The number of kilowatt hours used by Americans has increased dramatically since 1989. Although a couple of years showed a small decrease in hours used, overall usage has increased each year.	I can't believe that even with all the warnings about global warming and the loss of natural resources, people are still using energy to this degree! I know my family has tried to cut back some, but it doesn't look like many other families are doing the same thing!

After Reading

Make it a habit to return to a graphic to be sure you haven't missed anything.

F Pause and Reflect

First, go back to your reading purpose.

> • After you read a graphic, ask yourself, "How well did I meet my purpose? Is there anything else I need to learn?"

Directions: Answer your reading purpose questions.

What is the graphic about? *It is about changes in U.S. kilowatt-hour usage from 1989 to 2001.*

What does it show me? *It shows that electricity consumption has been on the rise. In 1989,*

Americans used 850 billion kilowatt hours. Twelve years later, they used 1,225 billion kilowatt

hours over the course of the year.

What conclusions can I draw from the graphic? *Americans are using more electrical energy.*

Reports that there is an energy shortage haven't really affected our use of electricity.

G Reread

Good readers are skeptical about the information presented. They don't automatically trust that everything they read is true.

> • Use the rereading strategy of reading critically to help you decide whether the information in a graphic is valid.

Directions: Take another look at the electricity graphic. Then, complete the Critical Reading Chart on the next page.

Graphics

Critical Reading Chart

"Kilowatt Climb"	
1. What is being compared?	Kilowatt-hour usage per year from 1989 to 2001.
2. What similarities and differences do I see?	The increase in kilowatt-hour usage is pretty consistent from year to year. On average, an additional 20 billion kilowatt hours were used each year.
3. Is there anything unusual about the way the information is presented?	No, although I'd like to see more recent data. I wonder if this trend has continued.
4. What trends or other relationships do I see?	The only changes in the steady increase in kilowatt consumption occurred in 1992 and 1997. I wonder why consumption dropped in those years?

H Remember

Putting into words the main idea of a graphic can help you remember what you've seen and learned.

- **Summary Notes are a way of helping you bring together the most important parts of a text.**

Directions: Write Summary Notes about the electricity graphic.

Summary Notes

Title or topic: Kilowatt-hour consumption from 1989 to 2001.

Main point: The number of kilowatt hours used by Americans has increased dramatically since 1989.

Smaller, related points:

1. In 1989, consumption was relatively low at 850 billion kilowatt hours.

2. By 1995, the number of kilowatt hours required by Americans had grown to 1,050 billion.

3. Rate of usage continued to rise. In 2001, the rate of consumption was at an all-time high of 1,225 billion hours.

Reading a Driver's Handbook

It is very important that you read your driver's handbook slowly and carefully. Your safety and the safety of others depend on it. The reading process can help.

Before Reading

Use the reading process and the strategy of skimming to help you read and respond to a state driver's handbook.

 A ## Set a Purpose

In most cases, your purpose for reading a driver's handbook will be quite clear: to prepare for the written examination to get a driver's permit.

- **To set your purpose, ask questions about the material you're about to read.**

Directions: Write three purpose questions for reading a driver's handbook. Then, make predictions about the text.

My purpose is to learn:

1. What is covered in the handbook

2. Which information is the most important

3. What I need to know to pass the written examination for a driver's permit

My predictions:

I think the easiest parts of a driver's handbook will be the section on signs.

I'm really familiar with road signs and symbols and what they mean.

I think the most challenging parts will be the rules when it comes to special situations, such as yielding to a school bus and an emergency vehicle. I have a hard time remembering when I should pull over and when I don't need to.

Everyday

B Preview

Preview to get a sense of the information you're about to read.

Directions: Preview these two pages from a driver's handbook. Make notes on the stickies.

Driver's Handbook

Most traffic crashes occur at intersections or in large parking lots that are open to public use, such as at malls and grocery stores. To avoid such crashes, you must understand the right-of-way rules and how to make proper turns.

RIGHT-OF-WAY

A **traffic conflict** is a situation in which a traffic crash might occur, no matter what the traffic signs, signals, and pavement markings tell the driver. An example of a traffic conflict is a car that is making a left-hand turn at a green light and a car that wants to proceed straight through. In this case, the two cars have a traffic conflict.

Our state (and all others) have a way of resolving traffic conflicts. We use what are called **right-of-way rules**. Right-of-way rules tell the drivers who gets to go first and who must wait.

*** *Here are the right-of-way rules and examples of how they apply on the road.**

* *A driver approaching an intersection must yield the right-of-way to traffic already lawfully using the intersection.*

Example: You are approaching an intersection that has a green light. Your plan is to drive straight through the intersection. Another vehicle is already in the intersection, turning left. You must let that vehicle complete its turn before you enter the intersection.

* *When two drivers arrive at an intersection from opposite directions at about the same time, the driver turning left must yield to approaching traffic that is going straight or turning right.*

Example: You approach a green light with the intention of making a left-hand turn. A vehicle approaching from the opposite direction plans to go straight through the intersection. You must wait for the approaching car and any other traffic to go through the light before you can make your turn. When approaching traffic clears or stops for a red light, complete your turn.

* *At intersections that are not controlled by signs or signals, the driver on the left must yield the right-of-way to the driver on the right. This is also true in cases in which two vehicles arrive at a stop sign at the same time.*

Example: You are stopped at a stop sign, and you are going to go straight through the intersection. A driver on the intersecting road has stopped at a stop sign on your right and is also going to go straight. You must yield the right-of-way to the other driver.

* *A vehicle entering a roadway from a driveway, alley, private road, or any other place that is*

NAME ....

Driver's Handbook

not a roadway must stop and yield the right-of-way to traffic on the roadway, as well as to pedestrians.

Example: You are driving down your driveway and have your signal on to turn left onto the street. In this case, you must yield to cars approaching from your left and from your right. If a pedestrian were crossing at the end of your driveway, you would have to wait for him or her to cross as well.

❊ *Drivers must yield to pedestrians legally using marked or unmarked crosswalks.*

Example: You are stopped at a red light. A group of adults step into the crosswalk just as the light turns green. You must yield the right-of-way to the entire group. You also must yield the right-of-way to pedestrians in crosswalks on your left or right before turning.

❊ *It is illegal to block an intersection. For this reason, you may not enter an intersection if traffic is backed up on the other side and you cannot get all the way through the intersection. You must wait until traffic ahead clears before moving into the intersection.*

Example: You are stopped at a red light. Ahead, there is a traffic jam caused by road construction. When the light turns green, you must wait until there is enough room for your vehicle to make it all the way through the intersection before you can proceed.

❊ *A driver entering a traffic circle must yield the right-of-way to drivers already in the circle.*

Example: You are stopped at a stop sign preparing to enter a traffic circle. Several cars already on the circle approach from your right. You must wait for these cars to pass and the road to be clear before you enter the circle. Keep in mind that this rule also applies to pedestrians crossing legally in marked or unmarked sidewalks.

What I learned from the headings: The subject of this section is right-of-way rules.

Boldface terms I noticed: traffic conflict; right-of-way-rules

I also noticed: There is a bulleted list of rules and examples. I guess these have something to do with right-of-way.

Everyday

Plan

After your preview, make a plan for reading. Choose a strategy that will help you get the information you need and remember what you've learned.

• **The reading strategy of skimming works well with most nonfiction texts, including a driver's handbook.**

During Reading

D Read with a Purpose

Remember that a large part of your purpose is to find the information you need to do well on the driver's permit exam.

Directions: Now, do a careful reading of the two sample pages from a driver's handbook. Write your Key Word or Topic Notes below.

Key Word or Topic Notes

Key Word or Topic	Notes
traffic conflict	A situation in which a traffic crash might occur, no matter what the traffic signs, signals, and pavement markings tell the driver
right-of-way rules	They tell drivers who goes first and who must wait in a variety of situations.
example of when you yield the right-of-way	If you are approaching an intersection in which a car is already turning left in front of you
example of when you have the right-of-way	If you are going straight and opposing traffic wants to turn left

NAME ....

Using the Strategy

You can use the strategy of skimming to help you prepare for the driver's exam. Reading tools, such as Study Cards and webs, will come in handy.

Directions: Make notes on these Study Cards. Then, write key details about right-of-way on the Web.

Study Cards

Right-of-way rules

Example of when the driver must yield the right-of-way

Rules that tell drivers who goes first and who must wait in a variety of situations

If you are trying to make a left turn and there is opposing traffic, you must yield.

Web

Pedestrians crossing legally in marked or unmarked crosswalks

When turning onto a public road from a driveway, parking lot, and so on

"Yielding the right-of-way"

Any approaching car if you are trying to make a left-hand turn

Vehicle to your right if you arrive at a stop sign at the same time

Cars that are in an intersection before you arrive

Everyday

E Connect

You'll have a better chance of remembering what you've read in a driver's handbook if you connect the information to your own life.

• Visualizing how you'll apply a rule can help you remember it.

Directions: Make a sketch that shows when you would yield the right-of-way to a car turning left. Then, make another sketch that shows when the car turning left must yield to you.

NAME

After Reading

After you finish the driver's handbook, ask yourself, "Have I accomplished what I set out to do?"

 Pause and Reflect

Ask yourself questions about the text and your purpose for reading.

• **Return to your original purpose and reflect on what you've learned.**

Directions: Answer these questions about the sample driver's handbook.

Looking Back

1. What is most important for you to remember from the right-of-way pages? If a vehicle in an intersection has already begun its left turn, then all opposing traffic must yield the right of way to the turning vehicle. But if two cars approach the intersection at the same time, the vehicle turning left must yield to the oncoming traffic.

2. What would you like to find out more about? I'd like to know more about other situations in which the driver must yield the right-of-way. For example, when do you yield to pedestrians and emergency vehicles?

 Reread

If you're not 100 percent sure that you've taken everything in on a first reading, you'll need to do some rereading.

• **A powerful rereading strategy to use with real-world writing is visualizing and thinking aloud.**

Directions: Write a Think Aloud in which you explain how you would make a right-hand turn from a side road into a traffic circle.

Everyday

◀ **Think Aloud** ▶

Well, if I'm stopped at a stop sign and am going to merge onto a traffic circle, I need to turn on
my right signal and then check for cars that are approaching from my left. If there are any, I have
to give them the right-of-way. I also have to check for pedestrians. If all is clear, I'll turn right onto
the circle and take the lane that is farthest to the right. Later, I can switch lanes if I need to.

 Remember

Good readers remember what they've read, especially if they know they're
going to be tested on the material later.

• **Asking "What if" questions can help you remember what you've read
in a driver's handbook.**

Directions: Answer these "What if" questions. Then, write two of your own.

◀ **Questions** ▶

1. What if you arrive at an intersection after a car has pulled into the intersection to make a left?

You have to yield the right-of-way to the turning vehicle.

2. What if you are pulling out of a parking lot at a green light, but there continues to be some

oncoming traffic? You must yield the way even if your light is green.

3. My question: What if you don't know who arrived at a stop sign first?

4. My question: What if a pedestrian crosses in front of you, but there is no crosswalk?

Focus on Reading Instructions

Almost anything you buy will come with a set of instructions. Some are quite easy to read, but others will be more challenging. The reading process can help.

Step 1 Set your purpose.

You'll probably have a purpose in mind before you pick up the instructions. Think about this purpose as you thumb through the text and diagrams. Mark the parts that you know you need to read.

Directions: What would your purpose be for reading instructions on how to store phone numbers in your phone's memory? Write it here.

My purpose: to find out the steps used to store phone numbers in my phone's memory.

Step 2 Read carefully.

Next, read the instructions and make notes. Use the strategy of close reading to help you understand the most important words and phrases. Read and reread these important details until you're sure you know what they're saying.

Directions: Read the set of instructions that follows. Highlight the most important details.

from *About Your Cordless Telephone*

MEMORY DIALING: STORING NUMBERS

You can store up to 20 digits including #, *, and PAUSE as a telephone number. Follow these instructions.

Pick up your handset. Press and hold MEM till a beep sounds.

Enter a two-digit number from 01–20. This will be the memory number for the first telephone number you want to store.

Press SELECT. The LCD displays the following screen:

```
          STORE NUMBER
3:16 PM                4/08


NEW CALLS 2
STORED CALLS 2
```

Everyday

> ### from *About Your Cordless Telephone*
>
> Enter a telephone number to be stored.
>
> Press SELECT. A confirmation beep sounds and the number is stored.
>
> The next LCD screen will prompt you to type in a name of up to 14 characters. Use the ⇑ and ⇓ keys to choose the alphanumeric characters.
>
> Press SELECT. A confirmation beep sounds and the name is stored.
>
> The LCD returns to Memory Store screen. To store more numbers, return to step two. To finish the operation, press MEM or simply hang up the phone.

Step 3 Think aloud.

As you read directions, it can help to think aloud.

Directions: Write a Think Aloud that tells the steps involved in storing numbers in a cordless phone's memory. Be as detailed as possible.

Think Aloud

1. I'll begin by picking up the handset and pressing the memory key until I hear two beeps.

2. Then, I'll choose the number that I want to use to identify the stored number. So, let's say I choose 01. I press "SELECT" and then type in the number I want to store. So, let's say I type in my home number.

3. Then I press "SELECT" again to store it.

4. Next, the LCD asks me to type in the name I want to "attach" to the number. I type in "HOME" and press "SELECT" one more time.

5. After that, I can end the program or store a second number.

Focus on Reading for Work

At work, you'll read a variety of texts. These will likely include employee handbooks, schedules, and memos. The reading process can help.

Step 1 Identify your purpose.

Think about what you need to know before you begin reading work-related materials.

Directions: Here, you'll read a sample of a company dress code policy. Imagine you are an employee of this company. What would be your purpose for reading the policy? Write it on the lines below.

My purpose: To find out what the company's dress code policy is and how it applies to me.

Step 2 Understand the organization.

A quick preview of the text can help you understand how it is organized. This in turn can help you find the information you need.

Directions: Preview the sample dress code policy on page 208. Make notes on the Preview Chart below.

Preview Chart

What is the subject of the policy statement?	Who wrote it?
How to dress at work	The Human Resources Department

Understanding a Policy

When was it written?	For whom was it written?
April 2002	All employees

Everyday

Computer Solutions, Inc.

325 West 87th Street
New York, New York 10103

April 2002

From the Human Resources Department
To All Employees
Dress Code Policy
Policy:

It is the policy of Computer Solutions, Inc., that each employee's dress, grooming, and personal hygiene should be appropriate to the work situation.

Specifically:

1. Employees are expected to present at all times a professional, business-like image to customers and the public. Radical departures from conventional dress or personal grooming and hygiene standards are not permitted.

2. Office workers must comply with the following standards:
   a. Employees should dress in a manner that is normally acceptable in business establishments. Employees should not wear jeans, athletic clothing, T-shirts, shorts, sandals, novelty buttons, baseball hats, or other items that do not present a business-like appearance.
   b. Hair should be clean, combed, and neatly trimmed or arranged. Shaggy, unkempt hair is not permitted.
   c. Facial hair of any kind must be kept clean and neatly trimmed.
   d. Tattoos and body piercings (other than earrings) should not be visible.

3. Any employee who does not meet the standards of this policy will be required to take corrective action. This may include being asked to leave the premises. Employees will not be compensated for work time missed because of failure to comply with the Dress Code Policy.

This policy applies to everyone.

The numbered list tells me the specifics about dress and hygiene.

What is the purpose of item # 3? It explains what may happen to me if I don't follow the dress code.

Step 3 Find out what you need to know.

Use the strategy of skimming to find the information you need.

Directions: Read the Dress Code Policy statement. Highlight key words and phrases. Make notes on the stickies.

Step 4 Apply the information to your own life.

Not everything you read in a workplace handbook, memo, or schedule will apply to you personally. But you need to find a way to keep track of the information that *does* apply to you. Making notes to yourself can help.

Directions: Imagine you are preparing for your first day of work at Computer Solutions, Inc. Make a few notes to yourself about the dress code policy. Write only the information that applies to you.

From the desk of

Dress Code at Computer Solutions, Inc.:

No jeans or T-shirts!

No sandals, but I guess boots are ok.

Get a haircut on Saturday.

Buy or borrow some conservative white or blue shirts—short sleeved and long sleeved.

Everyday

Reading Tests

The reading process and the strategy of skimming can help you answer the questions on just about any type of test you take. Practice the steps here.

Before Reading

Preparing beforehand is key to doing well on a test. On the day of the test, you'll set your purpose and then use the strategy of skimming to help you answer the questions.

 A Set a Purpose

No matter what type of test you are taking, your purpose will be to figure out what the test questions are asking and then decide what information is needed for the answers.

• **To set your purpose, ask questions about the test and test questions.**

Directions: For this sample test, you'll read a short excerpt called "An Anniversary Photograph." Write your purpose questions here.

My purpose questions:

What type of test will I be taking?

What are the questions like?

What is the reading passage like?

What is "An Anniversary Photograph" about?

What type of writing is it?

B Preview

Once you've set your purpose, begin the important task of previewing. If you're permitted, glance through the entire test. Try to get a sense of what the questions are like.

Directions: Preview the sample test that follows. Make notes on the stickies.

Midterm Reading Test

30 Minutes—4 Questions, 1 Essay

DIRECTIONS: Circle the letter of the correct answer to each question. You will not be penalized for incorrect answers. Write your essay in the blue test booklet.

MIDTERM REVIEW, PASSAGE #1

from *Thirteen Senses: A Memoir* by Victor Villaseñor

"An Anniversary Photograph"

The father sun, the blanket of the poor, was going down. The whole tribe of the Villaseñors went outside to have their picture taken.

Carlota, *"Tia Tota,"* as all the children called her, moved quickly with her cane in hand and took the main chair in the middle of the picture, sitting to Salvador's right and forcing her sister Lupe to sit on Salvador's left. And so this was how Salvador and Lupe's golden anniversary picture was taken, with *Tia Tota* sitting proudly in the center with her five-foot-two frame looking so large and tall and imposing as she faced straight into the camera.

Tia Tota really thought that she was the queen of the whole show, with her large, blonde wig, white-powdered face, and a huge white flower pinned above her heart area, wanting so desperately to hide her dark Indian blood and look All-American White.

Salvador was looking off into the distance toward his right, holding his black, thick-rim glasses on his lap with both of his hands. Lupe had one grandchild and one great-grandchild on her lap. She was completely oblivious to their picture being taken—she was so happy playing with these newest additions of *la familia*.

And standing behind Salvador and Lupe were their four children, Tencha, Victor, Linda, and Teresita, and their families.

It was a telling picture.

Passage #1 Multiple-choice Questions

1. "An Anniversary Photograph" is an example of what kind of writing?

　　A. expository writing　　　C. autobiographical writing

　　B. persuasive writing　　　D. fictional writing

Tests

Midterm Reading Test

2. In the phrase "large and tall and imposing," the word *imposing* means
    A. unhappy   (C.) intimidating
    B. angry   D. greedy

3. "The father sun, the blanket of the poor" is an example of a
    (A.) metaphor   C. simile
    B. alliteration   D. hyperbole

4. What is the author's attitude toward Tia Tota?
    A. He adores her.   C. He fears her.
    B. He despises her.   (D.) He understands her.

Essay Question
5. Explain what you think the author means by "It was a telling picture." Use
    details from the excerpt to support what you say.

I have this much time to complete the test: 30 minutes

I predict the reading will be about: Something bad happening while a couple is being photographed for an anniversary picture.

I learned this from the directions: I have to circle the correct answers. I will not be penalized for wrong answers.

I noticed this about the test questions: They are short. There seems to be a combination of fact and inference questions.

C Plan

Most tests contain a combination of fact and inference questions. Choose a strategy that can help you correctly answer both types of questions.

- **The strategy of skimming can help you find the answers you need in the shortest amount of time.**

When you skim, pay attention to:

☑ headings or headlines

☑ boldface words

☑ repeated words

☑ bulleted lists or text in italics

During Reading

D Read with a Purpose

A slow and careful reading of the whole passage or test item is absolutely essential.

Directions: Go back now to page 211 and read the passage entitled "An Anniversary Photograph." Underline important words or phrases. Then, summarize the passage here.

My summary:

The paragraph is an excerpt from _Thirteen Senses: A Memoir_ by Victor Villaseñor. It is mostly about a family grouping together for a photograph to celebrate Lupe and Salvador's golden wedding anniversary. One of the aunts pushes her way to the center. The rest pay little attention to the photographer.

Tests

Using the Strategy

Once you've read the passage, you can begin answering the questions. Read each question. Skim the passage for answers.

Directions: Read the four multiple-choice questions on pages 211–212. Highlight the key words in each. Then, tell where you should skim to find the answers.

Question #	Where I'll Begin Skimming
1	I'll reread the title and skim paragraph 1.
2	I'll skim paragraph 2 for this one.
3	I'll return to the opening for this one.
4	I'll skim the whole passage for this one.

Understanding How Tests Are Organized

Usually, the most challenging questions will appear at the end of the test.

Directions: Reread question #4. Then, explain which words and sentences in the reading provide clues about the author's attitude.

Clues I found: Tia Tota sitting proudly in the center; tall and imposing; queen of the whole show; hiding her dark Indian blood.

The author's attitude toward Tia Tota is critical. She is pretty pushy and likes to be the center of attention. He also seems critical of her because she tries to hide her true heritage.

Connect

Connecting to a test means thinking about what you've learned elsewhere and using what you recall to answer the question.

• **Connect to an essay question by recording your thoughts and feelings about the subject.**

Directions: Reread the essay question. Then, write what you know about the topic on the sticky.

Essay Question

5. Explain what you think the author means by "It was a telling picture." Use details from the excerpt to support what you say.

What I know about the phrase "a telling picture": I've heard this phrase before. It means that the photograph reveals a lot about the subjects' personalities.

 ## After Reading

When you finish taking a test, take a moment or two to think about which parts you feel you understood easily and which parts were more difficult.

F Pause and Reflect

When you finish a test, spend a moment reviewing your work. Are there any questions that you skipped? Are there questions you'd like to return to and rethink your answer?

• **Remember your reading purpose: To find out what the test questions are asking and figure out what information is needed to answer them.**

Directions: Answer these questions about the sample test.

Pause and Reflect Questions

Which question did you think was easiest? Why? I thought the first one was easiest because the answer is right there in the title of the passage. It's a memoir, which means it's autobiographical writing.

Which did you find most challenging? Why? The third question was the hardest for me because I always get literary terms such as metaphor and hyperbole mixed up.

Tests

G Reread

At this point, return to the most challenging questions, and try visualizing and thinking aloud.

- **Visualizing and thinking aloud can help you "see" the answer to a question more clearly.**

Directions: Reread the essay question. Then, write a Think Aloud that tells how you would answer it.

> **Think Aloud**

I know that this line about the picture being telling appears at the end of the passage, so I'll go

back and reread the line and the sentences that precede it first, before I do anything else.

Then, I'll think about where I've heard this phrase "a telling picture." I know that it means that the

picture is very revealing, as it shows the people's personalities. So, in my essay, I need to discuss

what the picture seems to indicate about the subjects' personalities. For example, I see that Lupe is

not paying any attention to the photographer. Instead, she is playing with the babies on her lap. I

think that means that she is a very maternal person. But does it also mean that she could care

less about the whole idea of a fiftieth wedding anniversary?

H Remember

You might be tempted to stuff the test in a drawer after your teacher gives it back to you, but resist the temptation. Spend a moment reflecting on how you did. Figure out why you had trouble in certain places.

- **Note which test questions you found difficult. They might show up again on another exam.**

Directions: Exchange books with a partner and grade each other's tests. Be sure to comment on your partner's Think Aloud.

I can improve my test-taking abilities by reading the test passages more carefully

and making more detailed notes as I read. I wasted a lot of time looking for answers to

questions because I didn't make notes about the most important parts of the passage

as I read.

Focus on English Tests

Often in English class, you will be tested on your vocabulary and your knowledge of grammar, usage, and mechanics. Follow these steps to improve your score.

Step 1 Preview.

As a first step, try to get a sense of the types of questions you'll be expected to answer. Then, mark any key words that tell you how to answer them.

Directions: Preview the three parts of this sample test. Underline key words in each question.

> ### Sample Test
>
> **Part 1 Vocabulary**
> 1. If <u>JECT</u> means "to throw," what does *reject* mean?
> A. throw to   B. throw again   C. throw back   D. throw under
>
> **Part 2 Grammar**
> 2. *The young children moved quickly toward the exit ramp after their teacher said "Hurry!"*
> In the above sentence, the word *quickly* functions as a(n)
> A. adjective   B. conjunction   C. adverb   D. preposition
>
> **Part 3 Usage and mechanics**
> 3. *My sister and _____ visited a museum last year.*
> <u>Choose</u> the word that <u>best completes</u> the above sentence.
> A. I   B. us   C. them   D. her

Step 2 Eliminate incorrect answers.

Next, eliminate the answers that you know are clearly wrong.

Directions: Return to the three questions. Cross out as many incorrect answers as you can.

Tests

Step 3 Use your strategies.

When answering vocabulary questions, use word strategies such as searching for context clues. When answering grammar and usage questions, use the reading strategy of thinking aloud.

Directions: Write Think Alouds for the three questions.

To answer question #1, I need to use what I know about word roots and prefixes to figure out what happens to the root "ject." The answer is C.

To answer question #2, I need to recall what I know about adjectives and adverbs. I know that most adverbs end in "ly," so I'm going to assume that the correct answer is C.

To answer question #3, I need to try the two remaining words in the sentence and figure out which sounds better. I think the answer is A.

Step 4 Figure out word relationships.

Save any word analogy questions for last. To solve them, figure out how the given word pair is related. Then find a pair that has the same relationship.

Directions: Read this analogy question. Make notes on the sticky.

odometer : distance :: _____

A. ruby : diamond   C. icing : cake

B. stopwatch : time   D. merciless : sympathetic

How odometer and distance are related: An odometer is used to measure distance.

The correct answer is B because a stopwatch is used to record time.

Focus on Writing Tests

Here's a plan that you can use to help raise your writing test scores.

Step 1 Read carefully the directions and prompts.

Your first step on any writing test is to read carefully the directions and the writing prompts. Underline information about the type of writing you're to do and the subject you're being asked to write about.

Directions: Read the following essay assignment and writing prompt. Underline any key words and phrases. Then, make notes on the sticky.

Sample Test

PROMPT: Your school board is considering a proposal that would add an additional school holiday to the district calendar. You have been asked to write an essay to convince school board members to vote in favor of this new holiday. What will you say to convince them?

DIRECTIONS: Write an essay in which you persuade your school board to add a new school holiday to the district calendar. Explain what the holiday would be, and then state why it is needed. Offer at least three pieces of support for your opinion. Be sure to proofread your work when you've finished.

The subject of the essay is: the need for a new school holiday

The type of essay I'm to write is: Persuasive (essay of opinion)

What I need to do to write the essay:

1. Read the directions and prompt.

2. Write my opinion.

3. Support it with evidence.

4. Proofread my essay.

Tests

Step 2 Write your thesis statement.

Your next step is to write a thesis statement for your essay.

Directions: Use the formula below to write an opinion statement for the school holiday essay.

subject
+
my thoughts and feelings about the subject
=
my thesis/thesis statement

new school holiday
....

+

it will benefit everyone
....

=

vote yes for a new school holiday as it will benefit everyone.
....

Step 3 Organize.

Take a moment to organize your essay before you begin writing.

Directions: Use this organizer to plan your school holiday essay.

Main Idea Organizer

My opinion: Vote yes for a new school holiday, as it will benefit everyone at the school.		
Detail 1	**Detail 2**	**Detail 3**
It will give teachers a much-needed break from teaching.	It will give students extra time to study for final exams.	It will allow for more family time, which will please parents.

Use a combination of personal details and details from other sources, including facts, figures, examples, and ideas from "experts."

NAME ....

Step 4 Write and proofread.

Put your thesis statement in the introduction. Discuss your support in the body of the essay. Finish with a restatement of your thesis or opinion.

Directions: Write a short essay on why for your school needs a new holiday. Proofread it carefully.

I believe that it would be a very good idea for the school board to create a new holiday. It would give both students and teachers a needed break. It would allow us to prepare for our exams and our teachers to relax after the semester's teaching load. There would also be more time for teachers to meet with students. One kind of benefit would be a chance for students to spend more time with their families.

All in all, the extra holiday can only benefit the school's teachers and students and lead to better scores at exam time.

Tests

Focus on Standardized Tests

Standardized tests examine the breadth of your knowledge in key academic subjects, including math, English, science, and history. The key to doing well on these kinds of tests is staying focused and reading carefully.

Step 1 Read the directions.

You need to read the test directions carefully. If you are permitted to write in the test booklet, underline key words and phrases.

Directions: Read these sample test directions. Underline any key words.

Sample Test

DIRECTIONS: Mark only one answer to each question. You will <u>NOT be penalized</u> for wrong answers, so it is in your best interest to <u>answer every question</u> on the test, even if you must make a guess. When you've finished with a section, close your book. <u>Do not move on</u> to the next section of the test until you are told to do so.

Step 2 Read each question.

Read the questions one at a time. Try to think of the answers to questions *before* you look at the choices given.

Directions: Read this sample question. Make notes on the sticky.

Sample Test

You can divide Shakespeare's plays into four dramatic categories. The categories are:

The question is asking me to:
name the four different types
of Shakespearean plays.

My answer: I'm pretty sure that
tragedy and comedy are two of
the categories, but I'm not sure
about the other two.

Step 3 Read the answers.

Next, read every possible answer to the question, even if you're sure you know the correct one. Eliminate answers that are clearly wrong.

Directions: Read the four possible answers to the Shakespeare question. Eliminate answers that are clearly wrong. Make notes on the sticky.

Sample Test

A. Comedies, Histories, Love Stories, Sonnets
B. Comedies, Tragedies, Histories, Romances
C. Comedies, Tragedies, Farces, Romances
D. Comedies, Tragedies, Histories, Thrillers

What's a farce?
Thrillers?

Step 4 Make an educated guess.

If you absolutely do not know the correct answer, make an educated guess. The strategy of thinking aloud can help.

Directions: Write a Think Aloud in which you explain the correct answer to the Shakespeare question. Explain how you arrived at the answer.

Think Aloud

I know that A is wrong because I know for sure that Tragedy is one of the four categories. I also know that D is wrong because Thriller is definitely not a category. That leaves me with B and C. I don't know what a Farce is, so I'm pretty sure I don't want to guess that answer. I'll say that B is the correct answer.

Tests

Focus on History Tests

Most history tests examine your ability to read critically, recall key facts, and interpret graphics. Following this four-step plan can help.

Step 1 Read each question.

Answer the easiest questions first, but be sure to read each question carefully, no matter how easy it seems.

Directions: Read this sample question.

> ### Sample Question
>
> 1. Which of these is NOT a reason for the fall of Rome?
>   A. Most Roman citizens were heavily taxed.
>   B. Small farmers could not compete with large landowners.
>   C. Diseases killed about one-third of the population.
>   D. The plebeians staged a revolution against the patricians.

To answer this question, I need to figure out which of the events did not occur or did not contribute to the decline of Rome.

Step 2 Rule out wrong answers.

Next, read every answer choice, even if you know the correct one. Eliminate incorrect answers as you go.

Directions: Return to the sample question. Cross out answers that are clearly wrong. Then, answer the sample test question on the lines below.

My answer is _D_ because *I'm pretty sure the plebeians never staged a revolution.*

NAME ....

Step 3 With graphics, look at the big picture.

You may want to leave the graphics questions for last, since these are often the most challenging. With each new graphic, ask yourself, "What can this graphic tell me?"

Directions: Study this graphic. Then read the question. Make notes on the sticky.

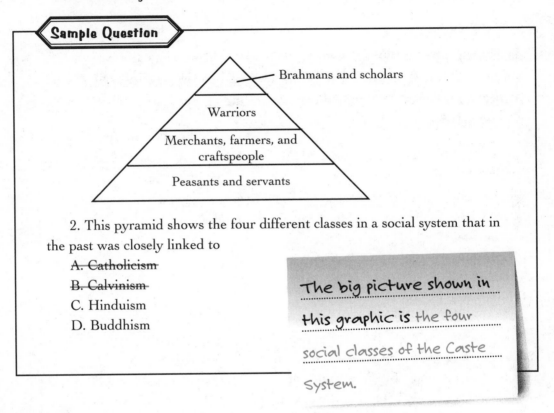

Sample Question

Brahmans and scholars

Warriors

Merchants, farmers, and craftspeople

Peasants and servants

2. This pyramid shows the four different classes in a social system that in the past was closely linked to

A. Catholicism
B. Calvinism
C. Hinduism
D. Buddhism

The big picture shown in this graphic is the four social classes of the Caste System.

Step 4 Talk through the answers.

Then use the strategy of thinking aloud to help you sort through the answers to the question.

Directions: Take another look at the graphic, and reread the question. Eliminate answers that are clearly wrong. Then, write a Think Aloud that explains the correct answer and how you arrived at it.

Think Aloud

I know that the pyramid shows the Caste System, and I know for sure that the Caste System had nothing to do with Catholicism or Calvinism. So I'll eliminate A and B. I'm actually not sure which answer is correct: C or D. But I remember reading something about Brahmans in India, so I'm going to guess Hinduism, which was born in India. The correct answer must be C.

Tests

Focus on **Math Tests**

You can do well on a math test even if math is not your best subject. The trick is to read each question slowly and carefully.

Step 1 Preview.

As always, preview the test before you begin writing. Mark the easiest questions with an asterisk. Mark the key words in the questions as you go.

Directions: Preview the sample test. Underline any key words in each question.

Sample Test

1. A child's pool holds 45 liters of water and it fills at a rate of 3.3 liters per minute. How long, to the nearest minute, will it take to fill the pool?

    A. 12 minutes   *too low*
    B. 14 minutes
    C. 15 minutes
    D. 17 minutes   *too high*

2. Last week at Millbrook School, 6 students were absent on Monday, 4 students were absent on Tuesday, 3 students were absent on Wednesday, and 7 students were absent on both Thursday and Friday. What was the average daily absentee rate at Millbrook for this week?

    A. 9 students   *too high*
    B. 7 students
    C. 5 students
    D. 3 students   *too low*

Step 2 Eliminate.

Next, read each question and its answer choices. Eliminate those that are clearly wrong.

Directions: Return to the sample test. Cross out the answers you know are wrong.

Step 3 Estimate.

If possible, try to estimate the answer. Check to see if there is an answer that is close to your estimate.

Directions: Look at question 1 again. Then estimate how many minutes it will take to fill the pool.

I estimate that it will take 13 minutes, so the answer to question 1 is B.

Step 4 Visualize.

If you get stuck, try to visualize what the problem is saying.

Directions: Make a sketch that reflects question 2. Then solve the problem.

Monday   🧍🧍🧍🧍🧍🧍

Tuesday   🧍🧍🧍🧍

Wednesday 🧍🧍🧍

Thursday 🧍🧍🧍🧍🧍🧍🧍

Friday   🧍🧍🧍🧍🧍🧍🧍

(6 + 4 + 3 + 7 + 7)/5 days in a week

27/5 = 5.4

The correct answer is C.

Step 5 Check.

As a final step, check your work. Use a different method to solve the same problem.

Directions: In column 1 is an equation you can use to solve question 1. Write a different way to solve the same question in column 2.

Equation 1	Equation 2
$45 \div 3.3 = n$	$3.3 \times n = 45$

Tests

Focus on Science Tests

To do well on a science test, you must be able to recall important concepts and use reasoning skills. The reading process can help. Follow these steps.

Step 1 Read.

As a first step, preview the test. Then, read the individual questions and any graphics.

Directions: Read the table. Think about the big picture. Then read the question and make notes on the stickies.

The Five Brightest Stars

Star Apparent Magnitude

	Brightness Factor	Distance from Earth in Light Years
Arcturus	–0.06	36
Canopus	–0.73	650
Centauri	–0.01	4
Rigel	–0.14	540

*The smaller the brightness number, the brighter the star.

1. What can you conclude about the relationship between the apparent magnitude of a star and its distance from Earth?

Stars closer to Earth have greater apparent magnitude.

2. Which of these statements cannot be supported with facts from the chart?
   A. Arcturus is closer to Earth than Canopus.
   B. Rigel is farther from Earth than Centauri.
   C. Rigel is farther from Earth than Canopus.
   D. Of the four stars, Centauri is closest to Earth.

The graphic shows five stars, their apparent magnitude or brightness, and their distance from Earth in light years.

I notice that both questions concern some aspect of distance from Earth.

Step 2 Read the questions.

Next, read the questions. See if you know each answer without looking at the choices.

Directions: Read the two questions on the sample test. Underline key words. Then, make notes on the lines below.

To answer this question, I need to use scientific reasoning to understand the relationship between the relative brightness of stars and their distance from Earth.

To answer this question, I need to plot the Sun and its apparent magnitude into the graphic and draw conclusions about its proximity to Earth.

Step 3 Use the strategy of thinking aloud.

Any time you're stumped by a question, use the strategy of thinking aloud. It will help you talk your way through to the correct answer.

Directions: Complete this Think Aloud for the two questions on the sample test.

◀ **Think Aloud**

For Question 1: I'll rank the stars in terms of their distance from Earth. Canopus is farthest, then Rigel, then Arcturus, then Sirius, then Centauri. Next, I'll jot down the apparent magnitude of each star. When I do this, I see that the stars closer to Earth have a greater apparent magnitude. This is the answer to the question.

For Question 2: I'll plot the four stars on a line segment to see which is closest to "0," or Earth. When I do this, I see that Centauri is closest, then Arcturus, then Rigel, and then Canopus. Next, I'll go through each of the four statements and see which is not true based on evidence in the table. I see that only answer choice C cannot be supported with evidence from the table. Rigel is closer to Earth than Canopus. So the correct answer to the question is C.

Tests

Learning New Words

Good readers know that mastering new words is important.
Focusing on unfamiliar words one by one will help you build
a better vocabulary. These tips can help.

Step 1 Read.

Watch for unfamiliar words as you read.

Directions: Read this paragraph from an essay about Ernest Hemingway.
Circle any unfamiliar words.

> ### from "Hemingway: The Old Lion" by Malcolm Cowley
>
> When Hemingway came back from the wars for the last time, in March 1945, he
> was the most famous writer in the world and he had chosen—or the public had chosen
> for him—the most obdurate problem he could bring himself to face. He must, the
> public said—and his friends took for granted, and Hemingway himself seems to have
> felt—he must write a novel about World War II that would be bigger in every way
> than his novel about the Spanish Civil War. For this he had more than enough
> material, all gathered at first hand, but there were obstacles to the writing of which the
> public and even his friends had no conception.

Step 2 Record.

Keep track of unfamiliar words by writing them in a vocabulary journal.

Directions: Record unfamiliar words from the paragraph in the journal on
the next page. Also, write down the sentences or phrases in which you
found the words.

◄ **Vocabulary Journal**

	English
	from "Hemingway: The Old Lion," p. 225
	Unfamiliar words
●	1. obdurate: "the most obdurate problem he could bring himself to face"
	Definition: stubborn or unyielding
	2. obstacles: "But there were obstacles to the writing"
	Definition: barriers
	3. conception: "of which the public and even his friends had no conception"
	Definition: understanding

Step 3 Define.

Use context clues, word parts, or a dictionary to define each word. For information on these strategies, see pages 666–681 in the *Reader's Handbook*.

Directions: Go back to the vocabulary journal and add definitions for the unfamiliar words from the Cowley paragraph.

Step 4 Use.

The best way to remember a word you've collected is to use it in conversation or in your writing.

Directions: Write one sentence for each of the words you defined.

◄ **My Sentences**

1. My parents were <u>obdurate</u> on the issue of changing my curfew.

2. My grandmother managed to overcome many <u>obstacles</u> in her life.

3. You have no <u>conception</u> of how difficult it is for me to cook a decent meal.

Vocabulary

Skills for Learning New Words

There are other ways to figure out the meaning of a word besides checking a dictionary. These include using context clues and word parts.

Step 1 Use context clues.

When you come to an unfamiliar word, try defining it by its context. This means checking the text that surrounds the word to see if you can find clues about the unfamiliar word's meaning.

Directions: Read this paragraph from Edgar Allan Poe's short story "The Fall of the House of Usher." Use context clues to figure out the meaning of the underlined words.

from "The Fall of the House of Usher" by Edgar Allan Poe

The disease of the lady Madeline had long baffled the skill of her physicians. A settled apathy, a gradual wasting away of the person, and frequent although transient affections of a partially cataleptical character were the unusual diagnosis. Hitherto she had steadily born up against the pressure of her <u>malady</u>, and had not betaken herself finally to bed; but on the closing in of the evening of my arrival at the house, she <u>succumbed</u> (as her brother told me at night with inexpressible agitation) to the <u>prostrating</u> power of the destroyer; and I learned that the glimpse I had obtained of her person would thus probably be the last I should obtain—that the lady, at least while living, would be seen by me no more.

Underlined Words	My Definition	Context Clues I Used
malady	disease	Previous sentence describes a disease.
succumbed	gave in to	Following phrases indicate that she gave in to the disease, or died.
prostrating	devastating	Since it killed her, the disease must have been devastating.

NAME ....

Step 2 Use word parts.

If you can't find context clues, check to see if there are any familiar word parts—root words, prefixes, or suffixes.

Directions: Reread the final sentence of the Poe paragraph. Then complete this word tree by adding words that have the root *tain*. Use what you've learned to define the words you've written in the tree.

Root Words

word: retain

definition: keep or hold on to

word: contain

definition: hold as contents

word: obtain

definition: to get (and hold) or to come to have

word: detain

definition: stop from leaving, hold on to

If you know the meaning of the prefix, you have a clue about the meaning of the whole word.

Directions: Add a prefix to each of the words on the list. Then, tell what the new word means.

anti-, ant- = against   *ir-* = not   *mis-* = incorrect, bad

Prefixes

Prefix + Word	New Word	Meaning of New Word
1. ir + *regular*	irregular	not regular
2. ant + *acid*	antacid	works against acid
3. ir + *replaceable*	irreplaceable	cannot be replaced
4. anti + *social*	antisocial	works against society; not in favor of being social
5. mis + *take*	mistake	incorrect action

When you add a suffix to the end of a word, you change its meaning and usually its part of speech. Suffixes can also give you clues about an unfamiliar word's meaning.

-ology = study of   *-ance* = action, state of, quality of *-ful* = full of

Suffixes

Word + Suffix	New Word	Meaning of New Word
1. bio + ology	biology	study of life
2. vigil + ance	vigilance	in a state of vigil or being vigilant
3. fright + ful	frightful	full of fright
4. confer + ence	conference	the action of conferring

NAME

Dictionary

Good readers have a dictionary at their side when they read. They are prepared to look up unfamiliar words. Without even realizing it, they follow these two steps when searching for the definition of a word.

Step 1 Read.

If you come to an unfamiliar word and can't define it on your own, use a dictionary. First, find the entry. Then read it carefully.

Directions: Read this sample entry. Then answer the questions.

> ### Dictionary Entry
>
> **inarticulate** (in' är tic' u lit) *adj.* not uttered in distinct syllables or words: an inarticulate mutter. 2. unable to speak in words; dumb: inarticulate with grief. 3. not able to put one's thoughts and feelings into words easily and clearly. —**inarticulately** *adv.* —**inarticulateness** *n.*

What part of speech is *inarticulate?* adjective

What is the adverbial form of *inarticulate?* inarticulately

Which syllables are stressed in *inarticulate?* "in" and "tic," with "tic" having the stronger stress

How many definitions does the word *inarticulate* have? 3

Step 2 Remember.

The easiest way to remember a new word is to use it again and again.

Directions: Write a sentence using *inarticulate* and another using *inarticulately.*

Sentence #1 If the speaker hadn't been so inarticulate, we would have been able to follow his explanation.

Sentence #2 She was so upset that she inarticulately motioned for the little girl to move out of the way.

Vocabulary

Focus on Using a Thesaurus

A thesaurus is a large list of synonyms. It is a tool you can use to expand your vocabulary.

Step 1 Read.

Your thesaurus can help you find synonyms for a given word. First, find the entry for the word in question. Then, read the entire entry carefully (antonyms are listed after the dash).

Directions: Read this entry for *futile*. Then answer the questions.

> **Thesaurus Entry**
>
> **futile,** *adj.* vain, useless, in vain, fruitless, hopeless, impractical, worthless, unprofitable, to no effect, not successful, to no purpose, unneeded, unsatisfactory, unsatisfying, ineffective, ineffectual, unproductive, idle, empty, hollow, unreal—hopeful, practical, effective.

1. What part of speech is futile? adjective

2. What are some synonyms for *futile?* vain, useless, in vain, fruitless, hopeless, impractical, worthless, unprofitable

3. What are some antonyms? hopeful, practical, effective

Step 2 Remember.

Using the synonyms you find can help you remember.

Directions: Use synonyms for *futile* to complete these sentences. Then use synonyms in five sentences of your own.

1. That is a useless idea. ....

2. She worked in vain. ....

3. The situation was absolutely hopeless. ....

4. She shut off the main valve to no effect. ....

5. They went on a fruitless search for the missing wallet. ....

My Sentences:

1. Jenny's plan to write both her midterm papers on Sunday was impractical.
....
....

2. The bully's threats were more than just idle.
....
....

3. Working on the wrong chemistry lesson was an unprofitable way to spend study hall.
....
....

4. Down by four touchdowns, the Giants game seemed hopeless.
....
....

5. After four hours, I ended the fruitless search for the perfect white shirt.
....
....

Vocabulary

Analogies

To complete an analogy, find a pair of words that explore the same relationship as the given set of words.

Step 1 Analyze the original pair.

As a first step, read the analogy carefully. Figure out the relationship between the given pair of words.

Directions: Read the sample analogies. Make notes on the stickies.

> **Sample Analogies**
>
> 1. bagel : bread :: rat :   2. rage : anger :: sadness :
>   A. mouse   A. fury
>   B. rodent   B. crying
>   C. trap   C. complaining
>   D. exterminator   D. misery

How bagel and bread are related: Bagels are a type of bread.

How rage and anger are related: Rage is a degree of anger.

Step 2 Explore possible answers.

First eliminate any answers that are clearly wrong. Then, explore the word pairs that remain. The strategy of thinking aloud can help.

Directions: Return to the sample analogies. Cross out any answers that are clearly wrong. Then, write Think Alouds to show how you decided on the correct answer.

Think Aloud

To answer Analogy 1, I need to find a pair that shows "a type of" relationship. So I look at my choices and eliminate D right away. It's clearly wrong. Then I ask myself, "Is a rat a type of a mouse, rodent, or trap?" Clearly the answer is B.

To answer Analogy 2, I need to find a pair that shows "a degree of" relationship. So I look at my choices and eliminate A right away. <u>Sad</u> is definitely not a degree of <u>fury</u>. For pretty much the same reason, I can eliminate <u>complaining</u>. Now I'll ask myself, "Is sadness a degree of crying or a degree of misery?" The correct answer is obviously D.

Step 3 Study.

It's a good idea to learn the most common types of relationships explored in analogies.

Directions: Reread pages 687–689 in the *Reader's Handbook*. Then, write an example for each type of analogy listed below. Write examples that are different from the ones in the *Handbook*.

◄ Relationships in Analogies

1. Antonym

flippant : deferential :: inflexible : bendable

2. Part of a Whole (Is a Part of)

star : constellation :: musician : orchestra

3. Item and What It Is Designed to Do (Is Used to)

scale : weight :: thermometer : temperature

4. Action and Where It Takes Place (Is a Place Where)

aquarium : fish :: lawsuit : courthouse

5. Result and Who Does It (Is Done by)

web : spider :: bread : baker

6. Class and Example of That Class (Class and Subclass)

flower : tulip :: tree : elm

7. Name and a Word That Describes It

chips : crisp :: lizards : scaly

8. Sequence

bulb : tulip :: first : second

Vocabulary

Author/Title Index

Photo Credits

23 © Photodisc

33 © The Natural History Museum, London

34 © Russ Finley Photography

35 © José Manuel Sanchis Calvete/ Corbis

86 © Bettman/Corbis

95 Courtesy Library of Congress

184 © Photodisc